CONOCIMIENTOS
PRESS

CROSSING BORDERS, BUILDING BRIDGES

◆

A Journalist's Heart in Latin America

MARIA E. MARTIN

CONOCIMIENTOS
PRESS

Copyright © 2020 Maria E. Martin
All rights reserved.

Published by Conocimientos Press, LLC
San Antonio, Texas

ISBN: 978-1-7351210-2-4

CONOCIMIENTOSPRESS.COM

Para mi Mami y mi Papi,
Charles and Adela Martin,
con mucho Cariño y Aprecio.

You gave me life
and made this story possible.

CONTENTS

9	**CHAPTER 1**	Crossing Borders
17	**CHAPTER 2**	Back to Central America: 2003
19	**CHAPTER 3**	My Central America Connection
24	**CHAPTER 4**	Starting to Report *Sin Fronteras*: Beyond Borders, 1986
29	**CHAPTER 5**	¡Ay, Nicaragua!
37	**CHAPTER 6**	Sad Return from Nicaragua
41	**CHAPTER 7**	On the Border: El Paso and *Latin American News Service*
45	**CHAPTER 8**	The Summer of Tiananmen Square and Curanderismo
52	**CHAPTER 9**	My Central American Experience Comes in Handy at NPR
55	**CHAPTER 10**	Leaving NPR With a Vision
60	**CHAPTER 11**	Connecting Continents: a Vision for *Latino* USA

64	**CHAPTER 12**	The Betrayals of Sister Dianna Ortiz
76	**CHAPTER 13**	Connecting with Journalists in Latin America
82	**CHAPTER 14**	Guatemala's Indigenous Peoples Pursue Voice, Meet Resistance
85	**CHAPTER 15**	From Latin America to *Latino* USA
90	**CHAPTER 16**	*Después de las Guerras* and Training Journalists
95	**CHAPTER 17**	Once Again, Starting Over
99	**CHAPTER 18**	From RadioGuate to GuateDigital
108	**CHAPTER 19**	Why I Live In Guatemala
112	**CHAPTER 20**	Rosa: The Warmest Heart
116	**CHAPTER 21**	Epilogue: Looking Back — 40+ Years
122	**ACKNOWLEDGMENTS**	

Chapter 1

CROSSING BORDERS

TO TELL YOU WHY I DO THE KIND of radio and journalism I produce I should begin by saying I was born in Mexico City ... My mother was Adela Garcia Ríos, whose family came from the Indigenous community of Texcoco and worked as household help. My father, Charles McGlynn Martin, was a *gringo* escapee from a cold climate. He'd ventured south from Chicago after World War II, to find sun and cheap living on the G.I. Bill. The son of Irish immigrants and the Mexico City gal together forged *una familia bilingüe y bicultural* — a bilingual, bicultural family — symbolic of the many connections between the United States and its southerly neighbor.

We lived in Mexico for my first six years; I spent the next six years of my life along the border in Arizona and Texas. When I was twelve, we moved to California. I start with this story of my beginnings because I don't think I would have the sensibilities and perspectives of the observer, the "outsider," the journalist, had it not been for living in two countries, and being the child of a bicultural marriage. In many ways, the borders I've crossed all my life and the bridges of cross-cultural understanding I've attempted to create through radio, all began right in my family.

In the 1970s, when I discovered radio (or rather, radio discovered me), being a journalist was the farthest thing from my mind. There were few role models in the media to encourage a Latina, even a bicultural Latina like myself, to aspire to a career on TV or on the radio. At least, I was not aware of any.

In my early years at school along the border, we were punished for speaking Spanish. But things were beginning to change in the late sixties and early seventies, as the African American Civil Rights Movement inspired another movement for cultural and political affirmation among Mexican Americans and other Latinos. As a university student, I'd changed my major from political science to Chicano studies. I joined a Chicana student group, *Mujeres por la Raza*.

One day in the mid-70s, in the wine country of northern California, I was absent-mindedly turning the radio dial when I heard something I'd never, *ever* heard before: it was in English *and* in Spanish. The station played reggae, rancheras, and *dedicas* (dedications) on the oldies show, as well as covered public affairs. For the first time in my life, I heard media that reflected my reality as a bilingual and bicultural person of Mexican *and* American heritage. What I was listening to were the sounds of the very early days of KBBF 89.1 on the FM dial in Santa Rosa, California — the first Latino-operated and owned public radio station. As Oprah would say, it was an "Aha Moment" — I was hooked on this pioneering little radio station and on making radio that cut across cultural lines.

In a few weeks, I wasn't just a listener of 89.1's "bilingual broadcasting," I was a volunteer producer for *Somos Chicanas*, a weekly talk show addressing Hispanic women's issues — probably the first radio program of its kind. Consequently, it was somewhat controversial. Birth control, women's sexuality, and abortion were among its topics. Women — especially Latinas, and particularly low-income farm working women — had *never* had the media address them directly. When they called in, they'd tell us they'd had to leave home to use the corner pay phone — God forbid their husbands should overhear them calling in to this *programa sin vergüenza* — this "shameful" radio program. I was then (and forty-some years later still remain) amazed by the power of radio and media to touch people's lives and make them act.

Maria Martin (left) and Mujeres of
KBBF's *Somos Chicanas* program, 1975.

One night in particular stands out in my memory: I was on the air after the *Somos Chicanas* program, hosting a music show. The phone rang, and at first all I could hear were sobs. In Spanish mixed with tears, a woman told me she was calling from the hospital. She'd taken an overdose of pills, but she wailed, no one at the hospital could understand her (in those days before bilingual ATMs and health workers).

The woman had turned to the one thing in this country she trusted — her radio station. This constant source of news and information spoke to her in *her* language, played *her* music, and was above all, her *lifeline*. Again, then as now, I was enthralled by the power of the microphone, the power of radio.

I think about that night often as I look back at how and why media — the kind I've done, the kind that hopefully has served to connect people, became *my* life. As the daughter of a Mexican mother and an Irish-American father, I've always felt deeply the need to bridge languages and cultures. Maybe I felt so strongly about KBBF and the power of media to build bridges of cultural understanding because, like that woman who called me in tears one night so long ago, I also needed a lifeline — one that would bring together my two worlds, my two Americas, with compassion and understanding.

In those days, the marginalization of Latinos in this country was a fact of life. Farmworkers, in particular, were second-class citizens — underappreciated and under-paid for picking the food on America's tables. In those early days of KBBF, much of its programming was aimed at Spanish-speaking farmworkers — many of them single men whose lives were often limited to long days of work in the fields and entertainment in bars at night. KBBF's programming, in Spanish and English, was their window into other worlds and an affirmation of their humanity.

Another pivotal experience in my radio life came about as a very green news volunteer: The news director at radio station KBBF handed me a Sony cassette recorder. Never mind that I'd never used the contraption before. Never mind that I wasn't really sure how to even turn it on. I was going to figure it out, because this was not just any assignment. This brand-new volunteer news reporter at community radio station KBBF, the Bilingual Broadcasting Foundation of Northern California, was going to a farmworker rally — and César Chávez, himself, the leader of the UFW, was going to be there!

At the time, Chávez had been trying to organize farm workers for over a decade — with some success, and with many struggles, just like everyone else in that Chicano movement. We'd followed the news about how Chávez fasted, marched, and boycotted. He was our Gandhi, our Martin Luther King, asking us to join *la causa*.

We were working on changing stereotypes of Mexicans and Mexican Americans and trying to improve conditions for *la comunidad* — especially farmworkers. And here I was, going to see Chávez speak as he tried to get workers in the wineries of the Napa Valley to join his union movement. As I got to the Napa County Fairgrounds where Chávez was speaking, the band started playing:

>*Viva la revolución!*
>*Viva nuestra asociación!*
>*Viva huelga en general!*

>Long live the revolution!
>Up with our union!
>Long live the general strike!

As the serious, dark-skinned Chávez addressed the crowd, I nervously checked the Sony 142: Was it still going around? My hope was it was taping what I thought was an historical moment.

That evening and the next day, César Chávez's speech at the Napa County Fairgrounds was broadcast on the radio — his words in Spanish inspiring and informing farmworkers and other new immigrants; in English, he and other second- and third-generation Latinos and non-Hispanics spoke about *why* there was a boycott, about what the conditions were like for farmworkers in this richest and most blessed of all countries. Again, it was the magic and power of a simple technology at work, giving voice to those who spoke to and for the voiceless. And serendipitously, I was in a position to broadcast what other media gave little or no coverage to.

For public radio to be truly of the people, I believe *all* voices must be heard—whether or not they speak the language of the mainstream... whether or not they fit into the demographic of so-called "core audiences."

My work has been rooted in the recommendations of the long-ago Hutchins Commission. Officially known as the Commission on Freedom of the Press, in 1947 the commission outlined the responsibilities of the news media in a democratic society, stating that it was the responsibility of the press to project a "representative picture of the constituent groups in the society." I believe this is at the core of a responsible press—that part of telling the truth is to reflect the society in all its many voices.

When I was at the University of Portland in the late 1960s, just a few years before discovering my radio destiny, I remember studying another commission's report. President Lyndon Johnson had created the Kerner Commission (formally, the National Advisory Commission on Civil Disorders) to examine the causes of the race riots that had erupted across the country. The commission's conclusion was that the media's inaccurate portrayals and misrepresentations of the African American community contributed to racial divisions in our nation.

In that then black and white America—as it was perceived—both the Hutchins and the Kerner Commissions urged the media to improve their coverage of minority issues. I firmly believe these recommendations are as valid today as they were when they were issued—and even more so as American society has moved beyond black and white, and as global reality dictates that we can no longer afford not to understand the "other."

According to the U.S. Census Bureau, by the year 2050 over 25 percent of the population will be Latino. As our country undergoes this dramatic demographic shift, it's clear to me that media—and public broadcasting in particular—have a distinct social responsibility to provide that "representative portrayal of society's constituent groups" that the Hutchins Commission called for decades ago.

And while I admire the work of those who produce the artful documentary or podcast, I perceive a greater need for radio and media to play a substantive role in bridging cultures and creating understanding through fair, accurate, and inclusive information.

This was the reason I left National Public Radio to start the program *Latino USA* in the early 1990s. As an editor on the network's National Desk, it was frustratingly apparent that even some of my very talented and educated colleagues lacked an understanding of the complexities of the Latino experience. Often, when Latino issues were even considered, the focus was on viewing Hispanics as "problem people"—i.e., with the dominant focus on stories about gangs and undocumented immigration. I wanted to create a radio vehicle that would portray the whole of the Latino experience, its complexity and diversity, its beauty and its pain. I wanted to hear the voices of Latino intellectuals, as well as people on the street, speaking English and Spanish and all the combinations in between, which gives such vibrancy and texture to Hispanic communities from Miami to Alaska. I wanted a radio program that would allow key audiences that listen to public radio to know that Latinos are not a monolithic group. I wanted to have a place on public radio for Latinos to feel at home—where Puerto Ricans could learn about Mexican Americans and Cubans about Dominicans and Central Americans and vice versa.

❖

The values of inclusivity, diversity, and the reflection of all society's voices have guided my four decades in journalism. These are the principles I've tried to uphold while working in public radio in the United States—at a number of radio stations and projects—including California Public Radio, the *Latin American News Service*, at National Public Radio in Washington as their one and only Latino Affairs Editor in the early 1990's, and at the project I founded in 1992 and headed for eleven years: NPR's *Latino USA*.

And, because it's always been clear to me that one cannot tell the Latino story without creating an understanding of the links that bind U.S. Latinos and their Latin American homelands, these values have guided the reporting I've done from Latin America — from Mexico, Bolivia, and Central America, in particular.

It's my hope that the memories of journeys through these lands give you something of what they have given me. To narrate this story, I begin with my return to Antigua, Guatemala, after having spent three decades in public radio.

Chapter 2

BACK IN CENTRAL AMERICA:
2003

I SIT AT THE LONG, handmade wooden table that's my desk in the small stone and wood casita I now call home in the colonial Guatemalan city of Antigua. My view beyond the balcony and the red-tiled roofs is of the perfect cone of the volcano called *Agua*. Water, like the autumn rains that come with such destructive force in this part of the world, causing hillsides to swirl and slide, bringing mud and rocks and misery to *la gente*, the poor people unlucky enough to live on eroded hillsides.

"What the hell am I doing here in Central America?" I sometimes ask myself. "So far from home?" But "home" is an interesting concept if you're a single woman with no children and tenuous ties to a father and siblings scattered among four states. Also, when you don't know what to answer when people ask about your origins. Is it Mexico, where I was born? Texas, where I spent most of a decade and a half? Or Guatemala, where I now live and work with rural and Indigenous journalists?

Often I think it's the view from my white stucco balcony — that vision of the volcano with its constantly changing appearances depending on the time of day and the cloud formations — that keeps bringing me back here, at this time in my life, to this place where I have no blood ties but that's been as compelling as if it were the land of my birth or where love has brought me.

Actually, it was radio, not love, that first brought me to Central America, just as radio has been the guiding hand in the fourteen or so moves I've made in the last quarter-century. Love? Radio? Maybe love of radio; certainly, love of what radio is, or could be: information resulting in action, in change, and maybe even in a little bit of a better world.

But when I arrived in Antigua, at the end of 2003, it was more like coming home to lick my wounds, to get over the scars of what really felt like battle. I was beaten down and hurting, with no motivation to do the work I had been doing with such diligence and heart since 1975. "Tomorrow, I'll start to work on this next project," I'd promise myself. No more putting it off. But my heart was not in it, even though I'd always been terrifically productive and hard working — to the point of being a workaholic, my friends would tell me.

Somehow, my motivation was gone — missing, disappeared. *La Causa* was not there anymore, the burning desire that had driven me for almost three decades. But to what? "To use the media as a tool for social change?" That sounded so trite and, really, if some of my former National Public Radio (NPR) colleagues heard that! Actually, some at the network already had accused me of: "Oh my God, 'advocacy journalism.'" What was it that an NPR program host had called me during my difficult years there? Ah yes, "the Latino advocate." I'd argued that reporting Latino issues was just as valid as covering a beat like sports, health, or science.

But they weren't buying that back then. No, not in those days, when it was permissible for big media to totally ignore the growing Latino population — in those days when the "correct" terminology about the makeup of the United States was "white and black," or" black and white." Never mind brown, Asian, or Native American. People of Latin American heritage were almost absent in the media, certainly in public broadcasting. To make them visible, I made efforts to have public radio live up to its name, and I gave it my all.

Chapter 3

MY CENTRAL AMERICAN CONNECTION

I HAD ARRIVED in Guatemala after the hardest chapter of my life, after I was forced out of the public radio project I had created in 1992, NPR's *Latino USA*. They say one door closes, and the universe opens up a window. And, so it was with this experience, although at first it was difficult to accept.

The path that led me here had actually begun many years before, prior to finding my life's path in radio. In my early twenties, my travels to rediscover my Mexican identity had taken me first to the land of my birth, and then farther south to a beautiful and exotic land even poorer than Mexico, with hidden undertones of unspeakable violence and darkness.

Later, in the late 1970's, I traveled to the Guatemalan city of Quetzaltenango in order to improve my Spanish. There I learned of student leaders being killed. I read with horror of cattle trucks full of Indigenous workers that regularly fell down steep mountainsides and were not commented upon, as if such deaths and injuries did not matter. I saw fear in the faces of the family I stayed with when I asked them about Guatemala's bloodstained politics.

It was around this time that I'd left my then job in social service to work full-time at KBBF as the station's very inexperienced news and public affairs director. It was 1978 and the *Sandinista* revolution

Inaugural event for *Latino USA*,
Bill Clinton and Henry Cisneros on the stage,
Maria Martin, May 5, 1993.

was surging in Nicaragua. On KBBF, under my watch, it was Nicaragua nearly all the time on our newscasts. For our sources, we relied upon English and Spanish-language news services as well as members of the Nicaraguan community in the Bay Area, many of whom had fled their country in order to escape the dictatorship of Anastasio Somoza.

While at KBBF I developed my first radio news magazine, *Mañana is Now*. It reported on, for example, the May 1978 massacre of more than 150 people in Panzos, Alta Verapaz, the first of many large-scale military operations against the Indigenous citizens of Guatemala. (In 2004, the United Nations would confirm that Guatemalan authorities were guilty of genocide, systematically destroying over 400 Indigenous communities.)

In the early 1980's, when conflicts in Central America were spreading and I'd become a news and public affairs producer at Seattle's KUOW, these conflicts were still hot topics. They were particularly significant to that audience, as Seattle was a sister city to the Nicaraguan capital of Managua.

I remember interviewing a very young Rigoberta Menchu — the Guatemalan Indigenous leader who would one day receive the Nobel Peace Prize — about what was happening in her country, and especially about the impact of so-called "model villages." Basically, these were concentration camps in which many rural Indigenous people were forced to live. Her stories about the government's targeting of Indigenous leaders and elders, of the loss of traditional culture, brought tears to my eyes.

I also put the very eloquent human rights advocate Mexican Bishop Samuel Ruiz of Chiapas on the air about the influx of Indigenous Guatemalans into Mexico to flee violence — at a time when much of the U.S. media was ignoring Guatemala in favor of covering the conflicts in El Salvador and Nicaragua.

Later, in between U.S. radio jobs, I traveled to Nicaragua to report and work with Nicaraguan radio stations. Returning to the U.S., I became the second English-language host and editor of the *Latin American News Service*, a ground-breaking bilingual reporting service based in El Paso, Texas. As part of my subsequent jobs at National Public Radio in the late 1980's and early 1990's (first with the program called NPR's *Latin File*),

I reported on the Central American peace process that slowly brought an end to the decades-long civil wars in Nicaragua and El Salvador. I also traveled south to report on the 1990 Nicaraguan elections that saw the end of Sandinista rule and the election of Violeta Chamorro.

My Central America connection continued while at *Latino USA*, when I traveled to Guatemala with my colleague, Susan Leffler, whom I had known since she had covered Central America for *Latin American News Service* and the *Christian Science Monitor*. Leffler would periodically travel from her home in the U.S. to Central America, particularly Guatemala. Often she would file reports for *Latino USA*. "One of these days, Susan," I told her, "Let's travel there together and do some special reporting."

The opportunity came in December of 1996, when, after nearly forty years of civil war, guerrillas and the Guatemalan government finally reached a consensus to end a bloody conflict that had taken over 200,000 lives and uprooted over a million Guatemalans, many of whom had fled to Mexico and the United States. The signing of the peace accords would take place over the Christmas holidays. I took time off to return to Guatemala for the first time in over twenty years and report with Leffler on the new developments.

Leffler and I filed a story for NPR's Foreign Desk about the first Maya mayor of a major Guatemalan city, Rigoberto Quemé of Quetzaltenango. We also produced a three-part series for *Latino USA* on issues related to the peace accords that would go on to receive a number of honors, including the *Overall Excellence Guillermo Martínez Márquez Award* from the National Association of Hispanic Journalists. The series won, not only in the radio category, but also as the "best in show of any medium," beating out reports from the *Univisión* Spanish-language TV network and the *Los Angeles Times*, among others.

My connection to Latin America runs long and deep. My work for the last few decades has focused on creating cultural bridges with Latin American journalists, and doing work that tries to educate public radio audiences about conditions in the lands of our Latina/o ancestors.

Maria Martin in Antigua, Guatemala.

Chapter 4

STARTING TO REPORT *SIN FRONTERAS*: BEYOND BORDERS, 1986

BACK IN THE MID-1980'S, long before I created *Latino* USA, and after working at the first Latino-owned public radio station KBBF in Northern California, at the state-wide network California Public Radio, and at Seattle's KUOW, I looked around for the next opportunity. "Where to now?" I asked myself, in this journey of trying to balance making a living with doing the right thing. Latin America again called to me.

A friend and colleague who'd started her radio career at Pacifica station KPFA in Berkeley, Isabel Alegría, was working on a San Diego-based pilot project for public radio called the *Latin American News Service* (LANS). After its initial planning phase, LANS had received operating funds from the Corporation for Public Broadcasting and was now operating from a new Latino public radio station in El Paso, Texas.

Alegría approached me about working on this project. The prospect intrigued me for many reasons. For one, I've always believed that one cannot tell the story of the U.S. Latino community without reporting on events in the countries from which many such Americans hail. In the Seattle area, for example, events in such countries as Chile, Argentina, and Uruguay were followed closely by a large number of individuals who had left those then politically troubled countries in order to find refuge. This same dynamic was felt in cities throughout the country. Wars were raging in Nicaragua, El Salvador, and Guatemala, with significant impact on neighboring Honduras and Costa Rica. These events in Latin America were having a profound impact on the U.S.

It seemed to me that the time was absolutely right for a project that reported, in both English and Spanish, events in Latin America to the influential public radio audience. I was also drawn to the LANS project because it was designed with Latino editorial control. Up to this point it had been my experience that — in general — Latino reporters, editors, and producers tended to have a greater understanding of the Latin American reality than their non-Latino colleagues.

So, in the fall of 1985, I packed up my umbrellas and raincoats from a nearly two-year stay in Seattle and said goodbye to the good friends I'd made locally. I stuffed my boxes of clothes, books, and reel-to-reel and cassette tapes into my 1979 black Volkswagen Rabbit. Then, I took the long yet beautiful drive down Interstate 5 to the San Francisco Bay Area, where I would touch base with old radio friends and colleagues, and prepare for the even bigger move to the border town of El Paso. I would start work there in the new year. As so often happens in life, events interrupted my trajectory and my plans had to change.

❖

Before the move to Texas, I had planned to spend Christmas with my parents in Guadalajara, Mexico. For the first time since starting in radio almost a decade earlier, I would not have to work during the Christmas holidays. Amazingly, I was not working sixty, seventy, or eighty hours a week. In fact, I was not working *at all*. I was between jobs and glad for the opportunity to spend time with my father and mother. It would be only the second time I'd visited them since they had relocated to Mexico, following my dad's retirement. They had visited me, of course, but those had been quick visits during which I could spend little quality time with them.

I had a lovely time with my parents in Guadalajara. Each day I'd walk in a nearby park in an effort to lose some of the weight I'd taken on during my stressful years at California Public Radio and KUOW, as I met

Martin covers week-long visit of renown Nicaraguan poet Ernesto Cardenal to the San Francisco Bay Area, mid 1980s.

resistance trying to make Latino issues more visible. I'd stroll with my parents near the condominium complex called *La Cascada*, where they lived. Yes, there really was a small waterfall gurgling into a pool below. The grounds were pretty and peaceful, with a garden incorporating dozens of rosebushes and other flowering plants. My mother was so very happy to be in her very "own" *casita*, something she'd always wanted. After years of endless moves and rented houses, she finally had a permanent home.

However, after a couple of weeks of restful and much-needed vacation, I became very ill. I was burning with fevers and racked with pain. A doctor — who, surprisingly, made a house call — told us he thought I had a paratyphoid infection. It could have come from the water, the doctor said, or from something I'd eaten.

"Why don't you stay here a while longer to get better?" my father asked. "Maybe they'll hold open the job in El Paso for you."

So, instead of starting at the *Latin American News Service* in January as planned, my illness gave me more time in Latin America itself. During my recuperation I did freelance reporting from Mexico for eight months, and afterward spent several months working in Nicaragua. During this time some of my reports aired on LANS as well as on *Enfoque Nacional*, NPR's then weekly Spanish-language program. I also freelanced for the Special Audiences division of National Public Radio on a bilingual documentary about the changing roles of Mexican women. This report came at an historic juncture, when the traditional roles for Mexican women were no longer limited to those subservient to men, when stay-at-home mothers, for instance, were being challenged on all levels.

I loved speaking with *mejicanas* in public markets and on the streets, as well as with well-to-do women in their fancy living rooms — *mujeres* old and young, gay, and straight. I wove their disparate stories using their words and English translations, along with the music of the great Mexican singer-songwriter, Amparo Ochoa. This was my third full-length documentary and I was beginning to get a good feel for this in-depth format, which eventually became my favorite mode of production.

Also, at this time, I was learning what it was like to work with U.S. editors as a "foreign correspondent." Often I found this to be a very frustrating experience. Many times, it seemed to me the editors I worked with were too attached to their own perception of what the story <u>should</u> be, even though they were in Washington or El Paso rather than where the story was taking place.

Another example of conflict was a constant debate over pronunciation. Should "México" be voiced as "MEX-ih-coh," or with its Spanish-language enunciation, "Méh-hee-coh?" Should one say "Nick-ah-rah-goo-ah" or "Ni-cah-rah-gua," as the name is said in more than half of the hemisphere? In both instances I favored the Spanish pronunciation, but was often overruled. These and other not-so-favorable glimpses into the minds of editors who guarded the gates of public radio's news about Latin America led me to make a drastic decision after I came home. I would travel south again, basing myself as a freelancer in Nicaragua. However, since I had learned through conversations with journalists in the region that it was likely to be difficult to report independent information when it came to Nicaragua's leftist government, I began to think that perhaps I could do more in Nicaragua than simply report daily news briefs.

For me, those months in Mexico comprised less than a year of linear time, yet they put me deeply in touch with many of the key social and political changes taking place in Latin America at the time. Being in those places opened by eyes even more to issues of social justice and social change affecting all of the Americas. This would take me to the center of one of the revolutions that was then brewing.

Chapter 5

¡AY, NICARAGUA!

MY FIRST INTENTIONAL "self-assignment" as a freelance journalist in Latin America was to Nicaragua. The year was 1987, I had returned to California from Mexico. Civil wars were raging in Central America. I wanted to see what was going on for myself.

These days, the Augusto Sandino Airport in Managua is modern and expensive. It's built of shiny white marble, not at all like the old airport it replaced, which was definitely in the Third World category when I first flew to Managua some thirty years ago.

"Where the heck are my two big bags?" asked the thirty-something-year-old Maria, here to freelance, produce an in-depth series of reports, and possibly teach radio to journalists living in this impoverished country. Most of all, I was going to see for myself what life was like in Nicaragua under the early version of the Sandinista government.

When Ronald Reagan took office as U.S. president early in 1981, his administration initiated a new policy toward the recently installed revolutionary authorities in Nicaragua. Two years earlier, after years of armed struggled, *Sandinista* rebels had toppled the government of long-time dictator Anastasio Somoza. These rebels had fought a long war against him in which thousands of Nicaraguans died, including many civilians who were bombed by their oppressive president.

The *Sandinistas* assumed power in a dramatic move that called worldwide attention to this so-called "banana republic." The move made many in the U.S. nervous about the possibility of more "Communist" takeovers in the region, long regarded by senior officials in the U.S. government as "their own backyard." Moreover, the propaganda circulating at the time held that Cuban and Soviet agents were infiltrating and financing the revolutions in several small nations in this part of the world: Nicaragua, El Salvador, and Guatemala. There was little admission that what was occurring in Central America might be populist rebellions against oppressive government policies, extreme poverty, and widespread corruption. Technically, what was going on in Nicaragua during 1987 was a civil war. As such, many who had supported the Somoza regime had organized a force of *contra* (opposition) fighters in a bid to topple the new *Sandinista* government.

At the time, the Reagan administration was bent on ousting Nicaragua's leftist government by financing an economic embargo and backing the *contras*. Seeing this first-hand and being in Central America in the mid-1980s was an experience that was to touch my life for years to come.

❖

At Managua's ramshackle airport shortly after my plane touched down, I nervously recalled that people often complained of lost and misplaced baggage. I began to think I'd be stranded without everything I'd brought in order to live in Nicaragua for at least a year — not only clothes, but other necessities I'd heard would be hard to get, including vitamins, tampons, and granola bars.

While waiting anxiously for my bags to appear, I remembered what President Harry Truman once said of Anastasio Somoza's father: "He may be a son of a bitch, but he's <u>our</u> son of a bitch."

By this time, Nicaragua had become a football in a geopolitical game between two superpowers, the Soviet Union and the U.S. "I've come to live in a country at war," I remember thinking. "I've come to make a home and to tell stories from perhaps the last battlefield of the Cold War." (Perestroika and the dissolution of the Soviet Union would occur four years later.)

At last, I found my luggage with its precious cargo and made my way to a rooming house in a lower middle-class Managua neighborhood that would be my first home in Nicaragua. Even though the fighting was taking place mostly in the countryside, life during wartime in the capital city entailed, among other things, food shortages, electricity blackouts, and severe water rationing.

Also, the grocery stores shelves were mostly and consistently bare. The lines for bread at local bakeries were long. It was a lovely day when, once or twice a week (if you were very lucky), the ice cream store had *helado de canela o de chocolate*. Cinnamon or chocolate flavored ice cream never ever tasted so good as during those hot and muggy Managua days.

For two or three days each week, there was no water at all. Forget that cold shower if you were hot and sweaty, which was the case most of the time. If you remembered to fill it the night before, you might have a little tub of water that you could wash with for the entire day.

I recall sitting on the back steps of the pink stucco *pensión* where I stayed when I first arrived. I conversed at length with young American and European volunteers about what had brought them to this war-torn land. Of course, I recorded these conversations — on a Sony recorder with rechargeable batteries that didn't hold a charge for long. But batteries were hard to get then in Nicaragua, so I made do.

Many were inspired by the romantic ideals of a leftist revolution that claimed to be for the poor and the outcasts. Others, like me, had come to see for themselves what the political debate was about. Still others were embarrassed by their country's proxy war against this basket case of a country and were trying to counteract the actions of the Reagan administration, which had positioned Nicaragua as America's greatest enemy. There were hundreds of such volunteers, whom, in a joking reference to their casual footwear, Nicaraguans named *Sandalistas*.

❖

My time in Nicaragua was in many ways most exhilarating. Every day I would meet a wide variety of interesting Americans and other foreigners who felt called to be in Nicaragua. The former included engineers from New Mexico trying to develop solar ovens to help poor families cook without totally diminishing the country's shrinking supply of firewood. There were digital information specialists from Iowa, Boston, and California teaching computer programs as a way to help the inexperienced Sandinista government.

Many others volunteered at the Finance Ministry in Managua. Outside help was especially needed since the number of empty desks in government offices throughout the capital grew each day. Some of those desks had belonged to Nicaraguans called to fight in the war against the *contras*. Others had left to volunteer to pick coffee in the plantations to the north, while still others had chosen to move to Honduras, Costa Rica, or the U.S. Some would never come back, victims of a war that eventually would take hundreds of lives.

It was at the same time a thrilling era of experimentation. People with interesting ideas could literally walk into a government ministry, talk to someone in charge (usually a former rebel in his or her twenties or thirties), and a while later have enough official support to be field testing ideas. The government was so new that there had been no time to develop the asphyxiating bureaucracy so common throughout Latin America.

In addition to freelancing as a journalist, I also did some radio production for an organization called *Tecnica*, based in the San Francisco Bay Area. I had first approached this group with a proposal for training radio workers in Managua. *Tecnica* responded with the idea of developing a series of audio profiles of U.S. volunteers who'd come to work in Nicaragua. I tried to convince them that this narrow angle wouldn't get much play on either public or commercial radio; that it would be seen as propaganda for the "other" side. Even on progressive Pacifica Radio, a series of one American after another saying the same thing seemed to me unmarketable. "Why not," I proposed, "a series called something like *Life During Wartime* or *Nicaragua at War*?" Such audio profiles would still feature some of the U.S. citizens volunteering — computer programmers, biologists, doctors and nurses working in the Health Ministry, for example, or those volunteering to resurrect the tourist industry. In my vision, these foreigners would be only part of these stories, not their main focus. The Nicaraguans with whom they worked would be the featured protagonists.

Tecnica agreed. And, so I gathered material for pieces about efforts to establish solar energy in Nicaragua and about the seemingly incongruous efforts to build a tourism industry in a country globally associated with war, death, and destruction.

After I'd sent material for four or five such stories to San Francisco, I received word that the administrators at *Tecnica* were not happy. There are "too many interviews in Spanish," they complained. In *Tecnica*'s opinion, I'd interviewed "too many Nicaraguans and not enough Americans."

Once again, I was flabbergasted by what I perceived to be the ignorance and lack of understanding regarding Latin America's reality. Even in oh-so-hip San Francisco, these liberals were not open to Nicaraguans telling *their own* stories. "Oh my," I thought, "I guess it serves me right for choosing this rather round-about way of describing the lives of everyday Nicaraguans. I guess it's not meant for me to finish this project."

The *Tecnica* job that unraveled was basically a volunteer assignment, paying me a mere $50 a month, plus airfare. *Tecnica* and I so differed about the focus of the productions that we soon parted ways.

Then, I considered what else I could do while living in Nicaragua. What I'd heard from many colleagues led me to believe that no matter what was actually going on in the country, reporters were often expected to send dispatches that generally lined up with the Reagan administration's view that the Sandinista government was an oppressive dictatorship and a pawn of the Soviet Union and Cuba. I did not want to have to fight that editorial battle continually through the filing of daily news reports.

My next step was to propose to NPR's Specialized Audiences unit a documentary about the "radio wars" then taking place in Central America. (This department was where most programming about minorities — and in this case *by* minorities about Latin America — was funneled.) I was excited by the ideas and the sounds I envisioned for this program. The war between the *Sandinistas* and the *contras* was not being fought simply with bullets, mines, and bombs. It was also a propaganda battle, both on the world stage and locally, for the hearts and minds of Nicaraguans. In much of Central America, people were giving up their lives for the right to control the means of information.

To begin my reporting, I traveled north of Managua to visit a radio outlet in the town of Ocotal, on the border with Honduras. I wrote in my notes: "The station seems to be very much about producing community programming — it trains people in the outlying rural areas to be community reporters and phone in news and cultural information." I learned that a few months earlier, this station had been attacked by the *contras* and several staff members had been killed. Again, I was struck by the reality that the microphone had power. This notion was much more striking in the middle of a situation that was truly about life and death. On the other side of the *frontera*, in Honduras, a powerful *contra*-controlled radio station beamed anti-Sandinista programming into the rural hamlets and towns along the border, doing its part to try and win this seemingly never-ending war.

❖

At the time, I also noted: "Nicaraguans everywhere are tired — of death, of the shortages and the sacrifice this war demands. *Campesino* (farmworker) families are tired of sending their sons off to die, on either side. Many families are divided: some supporting and fighting for the *contras*, others loyal to the *Sandinistas*."

As I traveled around and spoke to people, I became acutely aware of the war-fatigue that would eventually lead to the 1990 election ("the Super Bowl of the Left" as someone termed it) and the subsequent defeat of the Sandinista government of Daniel Ortega by opposition candidate Violeta Chamorro.

During my time in Managua I witnessed elitism and corruption within the *Sandinista* administration. While following a *Tecnica* volunteer working in the Forestry Ministry, for example, I had a chance to speak to a number of Europeans working there. They told me that their home governments, at first enthusiastic about the *Sandinistas*, were tired of the pilfering of equipment and other minor (and not so minor) instances of corruption that kept foreign aid from helping the people for which it was intended.

I also remember going to the *Casa de Cultura*, a community center intended to be a place where ordinary Nicaraguans could come to celebrate their traditional culture. After all, wasn't the revolution fought for the rights of such people? But after a number of visits I asked myself: "Isn't it strange how very few ordinary Nicaraguans are actually here?" It seemed instead to be a gathering place almost exclusively patronized by foreign *Sandalistas* and elite Nicaraguans of the *Sandinista* persuasion.

Such incongruities and ideological contradictions, along with the everyday reality that Nicaraguans began to tire of the shortages and sacrifices demanded of a relentless war funded by the most powerful nation in the world, eventually lead to the *Sandinista* downfall in the 1990 election. Still, I experienced lovely moments born of a widespread hope that a better society was being built. Perhaps the most important thing I learned was that when a people live each day on the brink of war that is as close as the next block or a province away, when there's a real possibility that death might be around the corner and almost every family has some direct experience with war, each precious day also brings an almost agonizingly sweet love of life. This permeates one's existence. Conversations seemed warmer and more poignant; music took on deeper, more resonant tones. Little things were imbued with special significance. Simple everyday acts became more meaningful. The poetry that I heard everywhere in Nicaragua seemed more moving when news of battles and shattered bodies were an everyday occurrence. War and death were close, but somehow their proximity made one appreciate life in all its many manifestations all the more.

❖

One day I was invited to an afternoon gathering in a house in my Managua neighborhood. The occupant was a daughter of renowned U.S. folk singer Pete Seeger. Seeger was visiting, holding court in the backyard, and acting like a regular Joe. Food was shared and conversations were lively. After the meal, people found seats on benches, stones, stumps, and wooden steps. Before long, Seeger took out his guitar and regaled us with an informal concert. I was sitting close to him and somehow managed to translate his lyrics into Spanish for non-English speakers in the audience.

Overall, as on this special occasion, my time in Nicaragua was both incredibly sweet and distressing. In later years, the country underwent many profound changes in its economy and government. Even the re-election of Daniel Ortega as president in 2007 could not take the country back to the promise of the left-leaning Eighties. Today busy shopping malls are a ubiquitous part of the Managua landscape, displaying every consumer product imaginable. Now, many people, including a number of former *Sandinistas*, cannot reconcile Ortega's 21st-century brand of authoritarian populist politics with the *Sandinismo* of the early years of the revolution.

As I write this, decades later, with another violent Nicaraguan revolution still going on, I remember my first stay in Nicaragua with a bittersweet mixture of both fondness and sadness. We have come a long way from the Nicaragua I had discovered in my thirties, when something as simple as a child's smile, a song played on a guitar, a breezy evening in a front-porch rocking chair, or a dish of cinnamon ice cream would fill one's soul with gratitude. Such were the little things that felt precious in the near company of death.

Chapter 6

SAD RETURN FROM NICARAGUA

THAT DEMANDING YEAR of 1987 was pivotal in my life and media "career," taking me to Nicaragua with plans to stay for at least a year. Although the *Tecnica* project did not work out as planned, there was other news to report on and many stories to tell in this vibrant land: thriving between life and death, enduring war and hoping for peace. But, the universe had other plans.

I had returned from the Nicaragua-Honduras border and was meeting with some *Tecnica* volunteers at a dinner club in Tipitapa, overlooking the large lake near Managua. Salsa music blared and there was dancing, another of life's simple pleasures that brought joy to daily living in a place often full of bad news.

My evening of fun was interrupted by an urgent message, I needed to contact my family. Immediately.

During the difficult call, I learned that my dear mother, Adela, whom I had left in Mexico only a few months earlier, had passed away. She was only sixty-six, not much older than I am at the time I'm writing this. Adela had been traveling with my father and a couple who were long-time friends. They were in South America, on a trip my mother had dreamed of for many years. The foursome had been to Argentina and Chile, then Brazil, which became Adela's last stop. Later I would learn that my *mamacita* had complained of a back pain. A hotel doctor misdiagnosed a slipped disc and ordered bed rest. By the time the doctors determined she'd had a heart attack it would be too late for her to get emergency medical help.

My own heart was filled with sadness, yet I felt disconnected from ways to assuage my grief. I didn't know whom to call. Even if I had, in Managua a phone call would have meant standing in line for hours at the post office in order to use a pay telephone. I also wasn't sure where my father was at this time. Was Charlie back at my parents' home in Mexico? Or still in South America? Over the next few days I attempted to get through to my brothers and sister with no luck. Later, I learned my father was indeed back in Guadalajara, at the sweet home he had shared with Adela for at least a decade. I made plans to go to see him, a decision that signaled the end of my Nicaraguan life.

I dreaded saying goodbye to the green stucco house in the Bologna District — with four wooden rocking chairs on its porch — where I rented a room from Sandra and Freddy Mejia. I would miss this young revolutionary couple and their two small children, Camilo and baby Carlos, both named after *Sandinista* heroes. By living with this family, I had learned of their idealistic hopes and dreams for their country.

While packing to leave, I was certain I'd return. I left behind some recorded material on cassette tapes, a suitcase full of clothes, and who knows what else, thinking I'd be back. Little did I know I wouldn't return to Nicaragua for many years.

❖

On my way to Guadalajara, I first stopped in El Paso to visit my colleagues at the *Latin American News Service*. This was where I'd been headed before life led me in a different direction.

One of my first stops in El Paso happened to be to a Safeway grocery store. Even though I'd only been gone from the U.S. for only a few months, I felt major culture shock. Instead of rows and rows of empty shelves, as in Nicaragua, it was just the opposite here. I found it emotionally difficult to deal with such an exaggerated oversupply of products.

"It's almost obscene" I thought. "Thirty different brands of each foodstuff, more fruits and vegetables than one can imagine, all shiny and artificially colored."

I felt almost embarrassed by how much we have in this country — and how little others have in places like Central America. I was even more embarrassed and ashamed at how the political actions of some of our leaders, along with our tax dollars, were largely responsible for people's misery and suffering, especially in Nicaragua.

My mother's death and the ensuing grief hovered over me like a dark cloud. I could not stop crying — especially when I returned to Guadalajara, where I found my father deep into drink and depression. I couldn't find words to console him. Here was the light and lovely apartment my parents had shared, its rose-studded garden and cascading waterfall now bathed in darker hues. Every neighbor seemed to participate in grieving the loss of their *madrina*, their loving godmother, in this small, close-knit community. I fit well in this caravan of sadness.

❖

Now I should note that, when I get depressed, in addition to my tendency to overeat, I also tend to be messy. I don't bother to pick up my clothes or put papers away. Such was the condition of the guest bedroom I had lived in so happily with my mother and father only a few months earlier. Now, it had become a real mess.

I was fast asleep one night when, in a vivid vision that appeared more real than a dream, I saw my mother standing at the foot of my bed: "Alive as you or me." Adela was wearing the blue bathrobe her *comadre* Lucy had given her.

Now you might think that if my mother came back from the other side, she'd have had an important message for me — something really life-changing and significant. But all that my darling Choochies — my occasional nickname for my *mamacita* — said was "*Maria, limpia tu cuarto!* (clean up your room.)" Well, I wasn't one to disobey my mother.

I took her words to heart and climbed out of bed in the middle of the night. I immediately hung up my clothes, then straightened out my books and papers and tapes. I felt so much better. I went back to sleep and awoke later with a little more peace of mind — not so mired in grief and depression.

As anyone who has lost a beloved parent knows, the grieving process takes time. Eventually I was able to leave Guadalajara for the Bay Area. I went ahead and accepted a renewed job offer from the *Latin American News Service* in El Paso, sublet my rent-controlled Berkeley apartment, and drove my little black VW Rabbit to the Texas-Mexico border. I started the job I had planned on taking a year and a half earlier — before life took me to Mexico and a cherished time with my parents, and subsequently to Nicaragua, to places that brought me healing, empathy, and understanding. All were places and experiences that opened my heart in important ways. While I treasured my times in Latin America, now the Southwest again became home.

Chapter 7

ON THE BORDER: EL PASO & LATIN AMERICAN NEWS SERVICES

I HAD RETURNED TO THE Texas-Mexico border — but not to the Texas border town of my childhood. This time, I would experience border living in the strange and almost magical city of El Paso, bringing back the reality of growing up in Nogales, Arizona and Eagle Pass, Texas.

My dear friend and colleague Angelica Luevano once told me, "Maria, you may not have good luck with men or jobs, but you certainly have good luck with houses." And, so it was in El Paso — after a stay of a few months in a temporary apartment — I found a magical place to live: the former carriage house of a large mansion on Oregon Street on the outskirts of the Historic Central District. Two large rooms made up this cozy two-story stucco fairy palace, white with blue trim on the outside, portholes for windows, and a wood-burning, pot-bellied stove for heat. Hand-carved oak cabinets with elaborate scenes graced the small blue-and-white tiled kitchen. My view from the small balcony along the upstairs' west side was Texas to the left, Mexico to the right. Outside the back door, a wonderland of mosaics decorated the yard I shared with my landlord and his family. The owner, artist Hal Marcus, painted iconoclastic border scenes and lived in the even more fantastical and quaint mansion that was the main house.

But alas, my not-as-good luck with jobs returned in El Paso. The young *Latin American News Service* (LANS), produced at Latino-controlled public radio station KXCR-FM, was destined to lose its funding from the Corporation for Public Broadcasting within six months of my arrival. It was a good thing that most of my furniture in the little magic blue and white *casita* was basic.

During my short time at LANS, I felt we offered a great product, true "radio in the public service." Each day we produced and made available two "feeds:" compilations of four or five reports from throughout Latin America, and even more if the news cycle warranted. One feed, edited and hosted by Angelica Luevano, was reported and produced in Spanish. The English-language feed was first hosted and edited by Patricia Flynn, whom I replaced after she was hired by NPR as an editor on its foreign desk. Among others sharing our two-room, T-shaped studio were Isabel Alegría, John Carrillo, and Claudio Sánchez, who later became NPR's stalwart education correspondent.

In my opinion, LANS was especially effective because we had Latin American reporters filing stories, as well as American and British foreign journalists. This provided us with a more nuanced context from which we could make editorial decisions. Among our correspondents were the late Alan Tomlinson, David Adams, David Gollub, Susan Leffler, and Martha Honey. Several of these reporters also filed regularly for NPR, the BBC, the Canadian Broadcasting Corporation, and the Christian Science Monitor. Among our correspondents for the Spanish-language feed were Julio Godoy in Guatemala, Oscar Ramírez in El Salvador, and Patricia Vásquez in Nicaragua. LANS staff had trained then-UPI print journalist John Burnett to become a radio reporter. He eventually came under NPR's radar and became one of the network's stars.

❖

This period of my life made me understand and appreciate even more the importance of an independent media operating in the public service. It's said that the news media plays a critical role in the construction of the debate over U.S. foreign policy, and that journalists write the first draft of history. If this is the case, I sometimes look back at this period as one of those eras during which the first draft of an important narrative regarding the U.S. and Central America was written. For those reasons, it behooves us to examine even more closely that accounting of a period from which Central America has yet to recover.

It's also important to include the role that was played by the alternative press. My experiences telling this story on the noon and evening newscasts at KBBF, on the program *Revista Latina* at KUOW, and at LANS are small examples of the role that alternative media — including the so-called ethnic press as well as community and public radio and independent networks such as Pacifica — played during a pivotal epoch in Central America's history. These outlets gave greater coverage, for example, to the peace movement and to the widespread resistance to greater U.S.-military involvement in the region, which was favored by hawks during the administrations of Ronald Reagan and George H. W. Bush.

As this country found out during the Iran-Contra hearings of 1987, the U.S. State Department had an Office of Public Diplomacy whose purpose was to shape public opinion on Central American policy. They did this in part by planting opinion pieces in various influential newspapers and by pressuring editors to get their reporters in line. Around this same time, I heard stories about certain State Department officials pressuring National Public Radio regarding its Central American coverage. According to my sources, this ramped up after NPR ran a story regarding a *Sandinista* funeral for victims of a *contra* attack. I also was told that on at least one occasion, then-Assistant Secretary of State Eliot Abrams called the network to complain after NPR's then-State Department correspondent Richard González ran a story regarding military aid to El Salvador. In contrast, the *Latin American News Service* and other alternative media were able to provide perhaps less censored versions of the history being made and written at that time.

Unfortunately, LANS was not able to provide this alternative journalism for long. Even though it was carried by at least a hundred stations, and had been recognized by the Corporation for Public Broadcasting with an award for its coverage, LANS's days were numbered. In 1989 plans were underway in Washington D.C. for another public radio project from a Latino perspective. Ironically, this would result in the demise of the *Latin American News Service*.

According to someone who sat on a Washington funding panel, that new project, proposed by NPR, was competing with LANS, which was up for renewed funding from the Corporation for Public Broadcasting. The proposed NPR program was to be about Hispanic issues in the United States. LANS, on the other hand, focused on *international* coverage. But, the panelists failed to make a distinction, and decided that the funding should go to the new project, to be called NPR'S *Latin File*. As a result, funding was pulled from a worthy Latino-operated project that provided a valuable service about Latin America to public radio listeners. In the end, what was funded became another divide and conquer strategy and a tokenistic approach to programming that eventually would fail.

Chapter 8

THE SUMMER OF TIANANMEN SQUARE & CURANDERISMO

ALTHOUGH IT WAS SAD to see a valuable project like LANS shut down, the period following closure of the *Latin American News Service* turned out to be an extremely creative time. Based on the border, with my reporting eye turned west to New Mexico, east to Texas, and south to Mexico, I had plenty of story ideas. Little by little, some outlets began to show interest.

During this time, I produced two personal favorites documentaries. One was a thirty-minute program on *curanderismo* — the ancient Mexican folk-healing art as practiced in Mexico and the Southwest — and the other a documentary recounting the legacy of Chicano political activist Willie Velázquez, who died prematurely of liver cancer at forty-four, leaving a huge vacuum as a political strategist and man of integrity on the Latino political scene. Because of the work he was doing promoting democracy in Latin America, that movement was also dealt a blow by his death.

❖

I pitched the idea for a documentary on *curanderismo* to the *Soundprint* series, a relatively new venture created by the legendary Bill Siemering, who'd played a key role in creating NPR's *All Things Considered* and in setting lofty ideals for public radio. In *Soundprint*,

Siemering had created a forum for longer-form informational programs produced in a compelling, sound-rich, storytelling manner: one that used the audio medium as "an art form to engage the listener's imagination and enhance the telling of a story: radio for between the ears." *Soundprint* accepted my pitch and even threw in some travel money. Now, I'd be able to produce the program I envisioned, featuring healers from Mexico, West Texas, and New Mexico. Perhaps I'd even be able to hire actors for the voiceovers and other "sound-art" aspects of the documentary I begun to conceptualize.

I wasn't working full-time, so I was happy for the decent pay — as I recall, something like $2,000 dollars plus travel expenses. Most importantly, I would be able to concentrate fully on this documentary. With *Soundprint*'s commitment in hand, I set up a makeshift studio on the second floor of my little blue and white two-story *casita* and got to work.

Toward that end, I traveled to the town of Porvenir in the dusty Chihuahuan Desert across the border from Fort Hancock, Texas, east of El Paso. I was to meet with a healer whose reputation ranged far and wide. As I wrote in the script, "Mexicans and Mexican-Americans, the poor and the not-so poor, dozens of people come from both sides of the border, six days a week, by bus and by car, to see the man they call Don Chuy, el *curandero*; Don Chuy, the healer."

His real name was Jesus Vásquez. People waited many hours to see him, some with serious illnesses and a great deal of faith. They waited on chairs lined up against the pale green walls of a large room. In one corner was an altar with flowers and statues of Catholic saints. Don Chuy himself sat on a couch on the other end of the room, where, when it came to one's turn, he'd use his hands and a pendulum to diagnose and heal. When I was called, he passed the pendulum and his hands over me, declared I had a "nervous condition," and prescribed various herbal tonics sold next door.

Some thirty years before the term "mind-body-spirit" became a catchphrase, my documentary spoke to that concept: "The *curandero* also helps the spirit," Chicana psychologist Concha Saucedo told me. My program would remind its audience:

> A lot of the illness we have (in this society) is illness of the spirit. . . . Some medical professionals are beginning to realize that this country's increasingly multi-cultural character calls for a deeper understanding of how other people view wellness and sickness. Native Americans, Southeast Asians, blacks, and other Hispanics each have their own healing traditions.

Eighty years old at the time of our first meeting, Don Chuy like many *curanderos*, came from a family of healers, and learned he had the gift of healing at an early age. This was also the case with Doña Gabrielita Pino, a healer who worked with herbs and massage in the northern New Mexico community of Buena Vista. Elderly yet spry, tiny Doña Gabrielita had an open and sweet disposition. She answered my questions and opened up a suitcase to show me jars full of herbs — herbs she had harvested to cure those who found their way down the winding, dusty road to her small adobe home.

Doña Gabrielita had so much knowledge that one wished for all the time in the world to speak to and learn from her. But alas, although I might have had more time than usual for this kind of production, I was nevertheless facing a deadline. Thirty-minute documentaries may require tens of hours of recorded material for that precious half-hour. The winnowing process is at first onerous, then painful, and always time-consuming, easily taking weeks to complete.

Nevertheless, there is a beauty to listening to these rich interviews over and over, while making decisions about what stays in and what, sadly, stays out. For me, this is a magical process where the spirits of those one has interviewed in some way guide the production. I worked on the *curanderismo* project in the studio of my friend Vicente Silva in the Barelas district of Albuquerque. The process was more than simple technical production. Maybe at that time I needed to hear these therapeutic stories of healing.

In the background, while I worked, the muted television showed scenes of confrontations between brave Chinese student activists and government troops in Beijing's Tiananmen Square. As the weeks of the spring and summer of 1987 dragged on, these initial historic democracy protests turned violent when, on June fourth, over 10,000 soldiers attacked the protesters. Television images documented the horror of the massacre of at least 500 civilians (some estimates say there were many more). Meanwhile, on the studio's speakers, the voices of Southwest and Mexican traditional healers spoke of cures for both body and spirit. How we needed healing then — and still need it now.

The resulting program, *Curanderismo: Mexican American Folk-Healing in the Southwest*, featured short "scenes" portraying various *curanderos*. Between these, listeners heard readings from Rudolfo Anaya's novel, *Bless Mi Última*, a classic of Chicano literature about a young boy's coming of age, guided by an Indigenous spiritual healer, a *curandera* named Última. I was fortunate enough to work with actors from La Compania de Teatro de Albuquerque, whose voices and readings gave the documentary a special character. This program is now a *Soundprint Classic* that can be accessed online.

❖

I can't recall the details related to the first time I interviewed the San Antonio-based Chicano political activist Willie Velásquez, but I remember being very impressed. He had a magnificent voice, and was funny, down-home, passionate, and authentic — and he spoke in an old-school *mejicano* style. Our initial encounter must have been at some gathering of Latino politicians in California in the early Eighties. With his clear and thought-provoking perspectives on the Latino political scene, Velásquez soon became one of my favorite people to interview.

I interviewed him on three or four occasions, as he traveled from his Texas base to California in order to organize voter registration campaigns and spread the word about the victories and efforts of his Southwest Voter Registration Education Project (SVRP). The organization was headquartered in San Antonio, but was establishing presence wherever there were enough

Latinos to influence the political scene. At this point there was a growing number of Latino elected officials in California, but at-large voting and gerrymandering often prevented more from joining their ranks.

In 1983, I was somehow assigned the task of chauffeuring Velásquez around for a day of interviews. The Reagan administration had just invaded the island nation of Grenada, and Velásquez spoke of his desire to extend his work of promoting democracy south into Latin America.

Everyone who remembers Willie Velásquez says something like this: "He had a passion and vision for democracy, he believed in the power of the Constitution to bring about a more democratic society." In 1986, I recorded a speech that reflected his staunch belief in the power of the Constitution to create social change: "I know that [it] is a live and breathing document," said Velásquez. "It's not a dead letter! Don't tell me it's a dead letter, because I've seen it work!" When I interviewed his colleague, the former mayor of San Antonio, Henry Cisneros remembered Velásquez as charismatic, yet principled and humble: "To watch him talk," Cisneros recalled, "was to watch a certain power — immoveable, certain, passionate . . . Willie never changed his style of dress — but wore those same khaki pants, *mejicano* shoes, and blue sport coat — and as a result the people called him Willie, just Willie."

Velásquez was born a butcher's son in 1944. He grew up at a time when Latinos were marginalized in the U.S., particularly in his home state of Texas. But, he believed that change could come through the ballot box. "*Su voto es su voz*," "Your vote is your voice" he'd tell Mexican Americans throughout the Southwest, as he walked precincts and went door-to-door registering Latinos. His slogan became the motto of the organization he founded in 1974. The Southwest Voter Registration Education Project started out in a small office in San Antonio, furnished with a folding table for a desk and a borrowed rotary telephone.

In fourteen short years, working with community organizers in hundreds of communities, Velásquez changed the political face of the Southwest. He did this through much hard work, but also with a huge faith in the fact that Latinos were just the kind of new blood that would help renew American democracy. Jane Velásquez, his widow, once told me:

He was always saying it was our turn now, *we* are the new immigrant class, even though some of us have been here for four hundred years, and some of us just came over last night. He felt that electing Mexican Americans into office was one thing, but (more important was) making sure that whomever we elected was going to be of quality, that we were not just substituting bad white officials with bad brown officials.

In 1988, Willie Velásquez began to feel an unusual fatigue. He was soon diagnosed with liver cancer—and died a few months later. In his short forty-four years he left a powerful legacy. When Velásquez started his push for change, few Latinos were elected to local, regional, or national office. However, by 2017, there were over 6,000 Latino elected officials across the country, according to the National Association of Latino Elected and Appointed Officials (NALEO). Moreover, the Latino vote is viewed by both major political parties as a force with which they must reckon.

None of this would have surprised Velásquez, according to his long-time associate, Andy Hernández, who told me that even as a young man Velásquez had an unshakeable vision regarding the potential for Latino political power. At the funeral, Hernández told me, somebody had mentioned that they recalled hearing Willy say, "It's inevitable that Chicanos are going to take back the Southwest politically . . . we'll do it because of our numbers . . . the question is not whether or not we're going to win, the question is what kind of politics are we going to accrue."

According to Hernández, twenty-five years later, Willie Velásquez was saying the same thing, and his central question remains unanswered—"What kind of politics are Latinos going to accrue"?

❖

After learning of Velásquez's death on June 15, 1988, I drove the long distance on Interstate 10 from El Paso to San Antonio to cover his funeral. Hundreds of Latino and other political leaders from throughout the country came to pay their respects, including then-Democratic Party presidential candidate Michael Dukakis. I called the News Desk at NPR to pitch a "spot"—a one-minute news report about the funeral and Velasquez's death. Alas, I could not convince the desk editor on duty that weekend that the story was newsworthy, even considering the presence of Dukakis!

I was livid.

If Velásquez didn't deserve a single minute on NPR, my God, what did that say about this "public" network's understanding of our diverse Latino communities? Other Latino reporters were also angered by this, and several wrote to NPR's decision-makers. Maybe this opened the way for my colleague, producer Alfredo Cruz and me, to pitch a documentary about Willie Velásquez to NPR's Specialized Audiences unit. In November, five months after his death, *Willie Velasquez: A Legacy of Political Empowerment* aired as part of NPR's Horizons series.

❖

Willie Velásquez clearly understood that opening up democracy for Latinos in the United States would eventually have an impact on many of the Latin American homelands. His organization had begun to make inroads into Latin America and was in the forefront of democracy promotion throughout the Americas—crossing borders, building bridges. In 1995, President Bill Clinton posthumously awarded Willie Velásquez the Presidential Medal of Freedom, the highest honor a civilian can receive. He was only the second Latino to receive the citation. I often wonder what Velásquez would be saying or doing about the rise of anti-immigrant sentiment under the Trump administration, believing as he did that immigrants continuously provided new blood and new life to American democracy and to the living practice of the ideals of the U.S. Constitution.

Chapter 9

MY CENTRAL AMERICAN EXPERIENCE COMES IN HANDY AT NPR

SOMETIME AFTER I PRODUCED the documentary on Willie Velásquez, I was offered a temporary assignment at NPR that became a full-time position. First as an editor at the short-lived NPR's *Latin File*, and then as the network's one and only "Latino Affairs" editor at the National Desk, I worked at the public radio network from 1989 to 1992. These weren't the easiest years of my life, as I attempted to make Latino and Latin American issues a greater part of the network's coverage. Nonetheless, these years made me appreciate my experiences covering Central and Latin America. As an example: I'd already gone to bed one Sunday evening in 1992, when I received a call from the News Desk at my home on Newport Place, a few blocks away from the NPR building. Riots had broken out in Mount Pleasant, a neighborhood in the Northwest quadrant of the District of Columbia. Apparently, the disturbances had begun after Latino residents had gathered to protest an alleged case of police brutality. A rookie female African-American police officer had shot a thirty-year-old Latino who'd been drinking in a park on that Sunday afternoon. "It's all tied to *Cinco de Mayo*," the voice on the phone told me. "Go and see what you can come back with."

That the incident was allegedly tied to *Cinco de Mayo* didn't sound quite right to me, although that Sunday indeed did fall on the fifth of May. *Cinco de Mayo* is associated with Mexican history, while most of

D.C.'s Hispanic residents at the time were of Central American origin — principally from El Salvador, Guatemala, Nicaragua, and Honduras.

When I got to Mount Pleasant later that night, tape recorder and microphone in hand, the rioting had quieted down. As I approached groups of young Latino men gathered on building stoops and street corners, I began to record the stories I had long suspected were true about that part of the nation's capital. The stories they told me underscored long-held resentment of Latino treatment by a mostly African-American police force. The men who participated in the riot, often young Central American males, had fled the violence in their home countries and now lived four or five together in one-room apartments — often working two or three jobs trying to make ends meet. In this atmosphere, on top of almost daily harassment from police, they told me, the shooting was *la gota que rebalso el vaso* or the drop of water that shattered the glass. Or, to quote an English-language idiom, it was "the straw that broke the camel's back."

According to accounts, the policewoman had ordered a Salvadoran man sitting on a park bench to put away the bottle of liquor he was drinking. The man spoke no English, however. Believing he had a knife, the officer shot him. Other accounts disputed her assertion about the knife, still protests — at times violent — soon followed. "Disturbances on the street, or uprisings, are not supposed to happen in Washington D.C.," José Sueiro, owner of the local Spanish-language newspaper, *El Diario de la Nación*, would tell the *Washington Post* twenty years later: "But it did happen on those two nights." On those evenings, I was on the street, talking to police and protesters and recording sounds among the thousands of Latinos who had come out to demonstrate. I heard the frustrations of fed-up young men familiar with street combat from their years fighting armies and police in Central America.

Some entire families participated in the protests, meeting at community centers and houses before marching into the night — in view of hundreds of armed police. They wanted peace, these participants told me, but they also wanted to take the opportunity to make their marginalized situations known. They felt nearly invisible in a city they now called home after fleeing civil wars. Resentment was boiling over issues of discrimination, unequal access to services, and difficult police-community relations and communications.

I drew a great deal of satisfaction in being able to report stories in the context I understood from having lived both in Washington DC and in Central America. I think I was also one of the first to report on another reality that the Central American community faced in this country: the lack of representation by national Hispanic advocacy groups such as the League of United Latin American Citizens (LULAC) and the National Council of La Raza (NCLR), whose membership at the time consisted mostly of Mexican Americans, Puerto Ricans, and Cuban-Americans.

The Mount Pleasant disturbances proved to be a wake-up call in many quarters: for the District of Columbia's municipal government (which soon began to hire more bilingual employees), for Hispanic organizations founded in the 1950's and 1960's regarding their need to be more inclusive of the changing demographics of the Latino community, and for the nation as a whole . . . coming so soon after the Los Angeles riots that followed the beating of Rodney King and the subsequent trial of the police officers involved. "This was also a wake-up for some people at NPR," I thought at the time. "Maybe this incident has made some of my colleagues understand the value of having a bilingual, bicultural reporter who knows the Latino community."

Chapter 10

LEAVING NPR WITH A VISION

DESPITE MY NEW HOPES for change at NPR, I left the organization with some trepidation in the summer of 1992. Even though I had high hopes for eventual change at the network, I also had come to realize that transformation can be extremely difficult for institutions, as well as individuals. I reminded myself, "I've worked here for three years. Finally, I've found some measure of acceptance — after jumping through hoops to prove myself, not to mention surviving attempts to get rid of me by certain people opposed to the idea of having a Latino Affairs editor on the National Desk."

In the end, the decision to leave came down to this: Out of about seven story ideas that I proposed, perhaps one — or two, if I was having a great week — would make it on the air. Of those ideas that made it to broadcast perhaps one wouldn't give me a sick feeling when I heard the final version. Those were ones for which I was not the editor, although some stories I edited were still questioned by my superiors.

"I have no mentor, here" I conceded. "I didn't attend the same schools as most of my co-workers . . . their editorial mindset did not include a Latino worldview." Hispanics employed at the network at the time for much longer than myself included one engineer and two reporters, each with their own stories to tell. The absence of Latino influential decision-makers and professional support at this level was both journalistically annoying and personally painful. Unless the Senior Editor backed a story proposal and took it to the editorial meeting or sold it to these shows, someone in my position was out of luck. A good number of stories I proposed had, in fact, died on the vine.

I recall writing a memo that detailed my concerns. "There was no coverage about a recent story on the alarming health problems along the U.S.-Mexico border described in the Journal of the American Medical Association, even when the Senior Editor knew about it and I had provided him with a list of people to interview." In addition, I cited the lack of follow-up on a number of other stories: hearings on the political status of Puerto Rico, Haitian protests of an FDA prohibition on their members donating blood, and employer sanctions connected to the hiring of undocumented workers.

While I loved the service aspect of public radio, I realized that making institutional changes that would yield true diversity in its programming would still be a challenging prospect. What if, I wondered, there was a project that would have a diverse audience, aimed at the entire American public about the Latino and Latin American experiences that derived from a Latino editorial perspective? This would be journalism that would reflect truth in its broadest form; a project that would continue a relationship with NPR and provide the network Latino-related content that would also be autonomous. *What* a concept!

And, so the project that would become *Latino* USA came into being when I connected with a group of people at the University of Texas at Austin who had approached the Ford Foundation for funding for a "Latino program." I consulted with them for more than a year to come up with a solid proposal for seed funding which I believed would lead to a viable program.

As a result of our efforts, the Ford Foundation accepted the recommendations and granted the project funding for three years. Sometime later, I was asked to produce a pilot of the program that would become *Latino* USA. I was then invited to apply for the position

Walter Morgan, Angelica Luevano, and Maria Martin, founding production staff for *Latino USA*.

of producer for this new venture. I lost countless nights of sleep trying to decide whether or not to risk losing a job for which I'd fought and suffered — one that was finally in the NPR permanent budget.

Finally, I took a leave of absence from NPR for a year. This was my safety net, as this was definitely a risky undertaking. Clearly, my charge would be complicated, as I assumed the responsibility of creating, executing, and soliciting funds for this project. Even my father, along with many others, told me I was crazy to leave NPR. But I had a long-term vision for what would become *Latino USA* and the important role it might play in public radio. When I met with NPR's then Vice President for News Bill Buzenberg, he promised me that if the project was successful, there was a "possibility" for the new show to become a Latino Affairs Bureau for the network. "I want," he told me, "to hear the pieces produced for your program on our air." In a letter to the network, on August 23, 1993, I resigned.

> *I do this with mixed feelings, as I very much value my relationship with National Public Radio. I am also well aware that the position I leave is an historical link to NPR's commitment to serving public radio's Latino audiences. I have great hopes, however, that Latino USA can be a vehicle for NPR to continue and expand that commitment. My decision has been eased only by my faith in the future—in the potential of Latino USA, in NPR's involvement with the project, in a vision that sees the talents and resources of these two entities utilized to create an exciting new sound for public radio, and to re-energize ongoing programming.*

After submitting the letter, I received a nice call from Buzenberg: "There are no doors closed at NPR," he told me. "Go make this thing work and come back."

Unfortunately, my hopes for greater investment by NPR in *Latino USA* were misplaced — for myself but more for the audience that public radio was meant to serve. Throughout the eleven years I produced the program, and even after that, I believe the network largely treated the project as a token stepchild, and did not give it the support it deserved.

Chapter 11

CONNECTING CONTINENTS: A VISION FOR *LATINO USA*

AS I TRAVELED TO TEXAS to start up the project that would soon be called *Latino* USA, I was in the prime of my life. At age forty, I was essentially starting over. I had both a hunch and a hope that the program would succeed and would be a significant vehicle in making public radio more public. Moreover, the program would serve to connect our Americas in a meaningful way. It would be all about crossing borders and building bridges, as in the Latino experience even if you are born in the United States of America, your parents or grandparents probably came from somewhere else and that is where your genetic memory may take you. Because when one talks about Latinos, one thinks of crossing borders: the ones at Eagle Pass or Tijuana, for example, or the many borders between Santiago and Seattle. A dry riverbed, an airport runway, or the cultural boundaries and traumas Latinos negotiate daily — these are borders, just the same.

It was my vision for *Latino* USA to reflect this reality. When we told the stories of U.S. Latinos in this country, we would also need to report on events across the continent: elections in El Salvador, the impact of immigration on communities in the Mexican state of Puebla, and Indigenous activism in Bolivia, for example. Our reporting would not stop at the Mexican border. Moreover, I wanted *Latino* USA to reflect Latin America from a <u>Latin American</u> perspective, not merely

Maria Martin in Bolivia with colleagues
Angelica Luevano and Selma Saravia.

feature the occasional report from a traveling American journalist with a "parachute" story where the reporter spends only a few days in a country, files a report, and then leaves. Thus, my vision — if that is the right word for an auditory premonition — was of hearing the voices of Latin American artists, academics, and everyday people, as part of the new voices that public radio would present on programs like Latino USA.

The long story of my time at Latino USA is one for my next book. Suffice it to say for now that for the eleven years I was its Senior Producer we made every attempt to have greater Latin American coverage on the program. We broadly reported immigration, not only from a policy angle, but also with human stories from U.S. communities and from Mexico and Central America. We featured stories from Bolivia, Peru, Cuba, Nicaragua, and other countries. Many of those pieces would go on to win awards. Through this work, time and time again, I was reminded of the gift and the responsibility we had with this half-hour of coast-to-coast airtime.

❖

After six years as the program's senior producer, principal writer, and editor, I felt the need to continue pursuing my educational career cut short twenty years previously, when I dropped out of Sonoma State University to "save" the country's first Latino public radio station when KBBF had run out of money and all its paid staff had left. In 1999, I was able to complete my undergraduate degree while still working full-time at Latino USA. I subsequently applied for and accepted a Kiplinger Fellowship to finish my Masters' degree in Journalism at The Ohio State University (OSU).

When I arrived at OSU in Columbus, eager to start my Kiplinger year with eight additional fellowship recipients, I had no idea the forthcoming experience would return me to Central America. This occurred when I was having a hard time deciding on a topic for my final investigative reporting project. In a conversation with one of my professors, he remarked: "You always light up when you're talking about Central America. Maybe there could be a project there."

And, so there was. Thus, I would return to the land that I love and would eventually choose as my home.

Chapter 12

THE BETRAYALS OF SISTER DIANNA ORTIZ

SOMETIMES A JOURNALIST'S ASSIGNMENT takes on a life of its own, becoming more than simply another radio feature. The story ends up making an indelible mark on the reporter. Such was the case with a two-part documentary series I produced in 1999, as part of my Kiplinger Fellowship in Investigative Reporting — *The Betrayal of Sister Dianna Ortiz* and *Surviving Torture: The Search for Healing*.

❖

I barely remember hearing the name Dianna Ortiz when her story first broke in the news late in 1989. At the time, my life was in a bit of turmoil, since funding had ended for yet another of the Latino public radio projects that employed me. As a result, I was no longer host and editor of the *Latin American News Service*. News from Central America — where conflicts raged in Nicaragua, El Salvador, and Guatemala — was a big part of what we had covered. Had I still been employed at LANS, I would certainly have been more familiar with the case of the New Mexico-born Ursuline Catholic nun who'd been sent to Guatemala to help the poor and teach Indigenous children, only to be abducted and tortured by the Guatemalan military. Following her release — a few days after she was kidnapped from a religious retreat center called *La Posada Belén* in the colonial capital of Antigua—Dianna Ortiz claimed an American called "Alejandro" had been present in her torture chamber. She asserted that he appeared to hold some authority over her captors. In response to this claim—and during the years she sought truth and justice—many people, including some officials of the Guatemalan and U.S. governments, called Ortiz a liar. And, worse.

At the time of her abduction the Guatemalan government was a well-known purveyor of human rights abuses as it conducted a brutal anti-insurgent military effort against several guerrilla groups fighting to overthrow the country's oligarchy. It was a campaign waged not only against the guerrillas, but also aimed at the country's civilians—principally Indigenous people living in rural areas. "If you cannot catch the fish, you must drain the sea," is what military dictator Efraín Ríos Montt is reported to have said later, in trying to justify a scorched-earth policy that destroyed hundreds of villages and many lives throughout Guatemala. Toward the end of the thirty-six-year-long civil conflict, as human rights abuses soared, in 1990, the U.S. Congress withdrew additional funding of the country's military.

Although the fighting had slowed down considerably by the time Sister Dianna Ortiz arrived in 1987, Guatemala was still raw with tension and suspicion. Based in the small mountain town of San Miguel Acatán, in the northern province of Huehuetenango, Ortiz was working with nuns who had been there for years.

The army was also there in force, keeping the population under control in a continuing effort to wipe out any guerrilla presence. After a while, Ortiz began to receive threatening letters, warning her to leave. They became so insistent that for a while she did leave. But, prayer and guidance reminded her that her mission was with the poor of Guatemala. It was shortly after her return that Ortiz was abducted and brutally tortured.

❖

Some years following Ortiz's release, she filed legal actions in Guatemala and the U.S., as well as before the Inter-American Human Rights Court. All this time, she experienced mental distress, and as happens with many survivors of torture, severe memory loss. For example, when she returned to her hometown in New Mexico, Sister Dianna couldn't recognize her family and friends.

Major news programs such as *Nightline* and *60 Minutes* featured her story but often the presentation was hostile, the questions skeptical. Media interviews often triggered the pain of her torture and caused Sister Dianna great distress. She was living through post-traumatic stress disorder and didn't know it. Sometimes Ortiz felt she was going insane, and other times, she wanted to die.

Sister Dianna's turmoil was aggravated by memories of what her torturers had made her do. In addition to enduring multiple rapes and more than one hundred cigarette burns on her body, the young woman had been forced to place her hand on a knife and hold it as her captors placed theirs over her hand, forcing Ortiz to repeatedly stab another female prisoner. The memory of what she had been compelled to do haunted Ortiz, as did what she felt were "betrayals" by some she had trusted, including several members of the press.

❖

So, as the focus of my investigative reporting project, nearly ten years after Ortiz's abduction, I followed up on her story. But, getting Sister Dianna to speak to me was no easy task. Surviving horrific torture, maintaining sanity, healing body and soul, and attempting to gain information about her case and pursuing justice had taken their toll.

I approached Ortiz's friend and colleague, Sister Alice Zachmann, the director of the Guatemalan Human Rights Commission USA in Washington, D.C. After many attempts to secure an interview, one day Zachmann informed me that she and Ortiz would be at the Cleveland Airport on an upcoming Sunday night en route back to Washington. Thus, on a cold and snowy November evening, I drove from Columbus to Cleveland.

The first time I saw Sister Dianna, she was huddled in a plastic airport chair. I was struck by her youthful and delicate demeanor. To me, she looked like a frightened teenager. Later I'd think, "She looks like a sad Virgin of Guadalupe, slight and brown."

It was clear to me that Ortiz had no desire to speak to me or any other reporter. In introducing myself, all I could do was say,

> I cannot even pretend to imagine what you've gone through, but I can tell you about something that happened to me. A few years ago, someone broke into a motel room where I was staying and tried to attack me with a knife. I fought him, and eventually he ran off. The whole incident must have lasted no longer than five or ten minutes, but those memories still haunt me in a way that's not really rational . . . I wasn't hurt physically, so I can't even imagine what recurring suffering your experience has left with you.

Perhaps this revelation played a part in her decision to let me formally interview her some weeks later. At her office at the Guatemala Human Rights Commission in Washington, I tried to be sensitive. She burned sage, which permeated the space with scented smoke in the Native American tradition. Sitting in a wheeled office chair, she would roll away from my mike, as she started to answer my questions. This did not make for great quality sound. I was torn between a radio reporter's imperative to obtain the best audio possible, and my compassion for her fear of microphones. Later, I would learn that during her torture she'd been filmed and recorded, while being forced to participate in the stabbing of a fellow prisoner. I decided I could live with the less than optimal sound quality, although I later re-recorded select parts of our conversation. For the follow-up I used a lavaliere microphone snapped to her clothing, yet I still did not have the heart to make her go over the sensitive and painful events of her torture.

Instead, I used a tape she had given me of past interviews with other reporters. She would write to me later.

> When we first met I was in a "fragile state." I had been betrayed, first by my government, then by a few trusted friends who had revealed sensitive information to the Department of Justice (DOJ) investigators without my consent . . . I wasn't at all certain I could trust you.

❖

I traveled to Guatemala during the spring break of my fellowship at Ohio State to further research the Dianna Ortiz story. "Why," I wondered, was this particular American woman captured and tortured by the Guatemalan military? Ortiz had been told that her case was one of mistaken identity, that they believed her to be a guerrilla leader named Victoria Hernández Ortiz. That didn't strike me as plausible. Sister Dianna, while Latina, lacks the Spanish fluency of a native speaker. There must have been *other* reasons.

Because my original plan to travel with fellow reporter Susan Leffler fell through when she became ill, I went to Guatemala with my friend David. Although travel in Latin America was new to him, it was a productive trip. In addition to advancing Sister Dianna's story, we reported from the Caribbean coast on the aftermath of Hurricane Mitch, and filed other news from the Mexican border and the mean streets of Guatemala City. This was taken on in a single week.

As for the Ortiz case, the spokesperson at the U.S. Embassy had little to add: "It was ten years ago, before my time . . . I believe nothing has ever been proven." Later, Thomas Stroock, who'd been U.S. ambassador to Guatemala during 1989, refused to speak to me on tape, but did say he thought Ortiz's story was "as phony as a three-dollar bill." For my documentary, I relied on previous public statements he'd made in earlier news reports.

During our trip, David and I made our way to San Miguel Acatán, the place in which Sister Dianna had resided. In the regional capital of Huehuetenango, we rented a jeep and hired a driver to take us up a narrow dirt road into the Cuchumatanes Mountains. According to the driver, the trip would take several hours. Even leaving at dawn, our time in San Miguel was restricted. He informed us there'd been many reports of bandits on the roads and he wanted to make sure we came back before dark.

My subsequent radio report on the Ortiz case started with the sound of our rented jeep driving up the mountain road and my voiceover: "It's not easy to get to San Miguel Acatán." During the drive, David and I held our collective breath as we looked down the sides of scary and impressive slopes — the Cuchumatanes are the highest range in Central America. The driver would nonchalantly identify points of interest along the way: "*Aquí es donde se cayó la camioneta de la Coca-Cola . . .*" ("This is where the Coca-Cola truck went over . . .") For his comfort, I didn't translate for David, who already looked rather ashen.

Arriving in San Miguel, we made our way to the white church that marks the center of the town, only to find the priest away on visits to outlying communities. (Those days, there were no phones in San Miguel.) But a kind assistant showed us around the church and the brightly colored school next door, built around a flower garden and a statue of the Virgin Mary. That was the place where Dianna taught the area's children; it had been renamed in her honor *La Escuela Parochial Dianna Ortiz* — the Dianna Ortiz Parochial School. A worker at the school told me, "this community knew and admired Ortiz very much and that's why they named the school after her."

We had arrived during Holy Week, which meant many San Miguel residents were not working in their fields, but instead were attending a religious workshop. Shaded from the sun beneath the corrugated metal of a large pagoda, they sat on wooden benches. David and I found an empty bench and listened to the presentation in the local Mayan dialect by parish sacristan Chico Martin. During a break, I took the opportunity to speak to the sacristan. I let him know who we were and explained that we hoped to speak to some of the parishioners who knew Sister Dianna. Sacristan Martin immediately handed me his megaphone. I quickly thought about ways to approach and gain the trust of people who had seen a lot of violence, and would naturally be suspicious of strangers. Even though the war was technically over, I was certain that their scars, like Sister Dianna's, had likely not healed. I didn't want to scare them off, yet I didn't have much time to secure their trust.

"*Buenas tardes*," I began. Then, I introduced myself as a *radioperiodista* who wanted to tell the story of someone who once lived in their town. I told them I knew Sister Dianna Ortiz, the woman after which they'd named their local school, and that I brought *saludos* (greetings) from her. I added that if anyone wanted to send a message to Sister Dianna, I would be happy to record it and deliver it. I took a deep breath and waited to see what reaction my request would have from the *San Migueleños*.

Surprisingly, I couldn't have had a more perfect response from the crowd. People lined up in droves to speak with me, especially mothers carrying their children. They sent their love to Sister Dianna, and told her of having had to leave San Miguel because of the violence to go into exile in Mexico. Some mothers said they named their daughters Dianna in her honor — they expressed how much they missed her, and spoke about what she meant to them. My recorder was rolling, and I took photographs to give to Ortiz.

When I finished recording their *testimonios*, a group of children stood up and loudly cheered with gusto: "Se oye, se siente, *Dianna Ortiz está presente*." They wanted the world to know that "you can hear it, you can feel it," because Dianna Ortiz's spirit was always present.

When I got home to Ohio, the first thing I would do was to make cassette tape copies of these "testimonials" and send them, along with photos of the people of San Miguel, to Ortiz. Sister Alice Zachmann would later tell me how important these would be to Sister Dianna's healing as a torture survivor. Zachmann conveyed that, although Ortiz's memory of events in Guatemala remained shaky, she believed Sister Dianna seemed to feel that "somehow she had brought shame on the people of San Miguel," adding that "these (keepsakes from my visit) would help her get over that."

One of the residents who had named his daughter Dianna was sacristan Chico Martin. My interview with him was also significant. "Sister Dianna started the youth ministry and helped the young people a lot during the time of the violence," he offered, adding that, "she supported the young men who were forcibly recruited to go into the army." With this conversation with Martin, I gained a sense of what had placed Ortiz in danger ten years earlier. I pictured a brave young nun, courageous enough to go before the area's military commander to plead to have some of the town's young men excused from military service because, for instance, they were the sole support of a widowed mother, or were the only male child.

From my experience of the *machista*, misogynistic, and traditionally racist Guatemalan culture, I was able to intuit how this could have been received. Not only was Sister Dianna a Catholic nun, at a time when many Catholic clergy were considered radical and often persecuted, she also was a woman in a male-dominated society. What is more, she was brown, with Indigenous features, in a country where racial discrimination is rampant. Thus, when she dared to challenge the all-powerful military in this isolated community, I understood the great danger in which she found herself.

❖

The reporting trip to Guatemala took place in April of 1999 and was followed that summer by my other Ortiz-related investigations and interviews. I returned to Texas and *Latino* USA in September to finish production of this investigative project. One of the interviews I completed was with a former Drug Enforcement Agency special operative named Celerino Castillo, who'd been based in Central America from 1985 to 1990 — during the time of Sister Dianna's abduction. I asked Castillo whether he knew of any internal investigation by U.S. Embassy personnel to determine the possible identity of the man whom Ortiz had identified as an American in her torture chamber named "Alejandro."

"No, not all," said Castillo. He continued,

> This (was) business as usual. These things happened all the time . . . The case of Dianna Ortiz was just one of them involving Americans. Nobody's going to go around asking, "Hey did you guys know anything or did you hear anything from your informants and so forth," because they knew exactly how it had occurred and how it happened and who had financed the whole operation, which was the Guatemalan military. Those (were) our counterparts that we worked with in Guatemala.

Castillo had been a source in previous news stories detailing how, at the time, the U.S. cooperated in Guatemala with a government whose security forces routinely used torture and murder to accomplish their goals.

The broadcast date was scheduled for November, the tenth anniversary of Ortiz's abduction. However, my deadline came before I was able to get any further evidence on the existence of "Alejandro." Yet, expert sources told me there were analogous cases of U.S. personnel, mostly CIA agents, being present in foreign prisons when victims were tortured, as in the case of an Honduran named Inez Murillo, whose story appeared in the *Baltimore Sun*. It documented Murillo's assertion that a person with an American accent had been present, if not during her torture, then while Murillo was blindfolded and showed signs of having been beaten and abused. National Security Archives policy analyst Kate Doyle, an expert on U.S. involvement in Guatemala, asked rhetorically during an interview: "When you are trying to weigh Dianna's assertions . . . is this absurd that this Alejandro (was present)? Well, there have been cases in which this was known to have been true. So, it is not at all absurd, it is not at all impossible."

❖

In many ways, this was my most ambitious documentary. It was a labor of love and also posed a challenge. How do you make written documents come alive in a radio piece without boring your audience? I decided to use the compelling voices of colleagues John Ailie and Angelica Luevano reading sections of pertinent documents in both English and Spanish. I also relied on elements that make for great radio, in this case including the ambient sound of a young nun's choir recorded at *La Posada Belén* where Ortiz had been abducted.

For whatever reasons, the documentary found a favorable critical audience and won several important awards. I remember the thrill of hearing a recording on my telephone answering machine: "Maria, this is Ethel Kennedy, and I am calling to congratulate you on winning the Robert F. Kennedy Journalism Award." The ceremony, held near Washington, D.C., felt like a dream. Many Kennedy and Cuomo family members were in attendance, as well as journalists such as Diane Sawyer and Geraldo Rivera. But for me the most significant part of this evening was the attention showered on Sister Dianna Ortiz, who accompanied me, along with Sister Alice Zachmann. It was, I believe, an affirming experience for her after so many years of feeling betrayed in her quest for justice and truth by the press and government agencies.

Sometime later I received a letter from Sister Dianna. It's something I have come to treasure even more than the awards I received for telling her story. In her words, Sister Dianna writes,

> *Years ago, a survivor friend told me during one of our conversations that the only people he would trust would be those who had themselves been tortured. "Those who claim to be your friends," he told me, "will betray you." His bleak words really disturbed me, but I refused to believe them. I knew that one of the objectives of torture was to destroy a person's trust in humanity. I wanted to believe that my torturers were not successful in destroying my trust in the human family. But the betrayals reminded me of my friend's words. He had tried to warn me but my naiveté and tenacity blinded me from seeing the truth.*

Ethel Kennedy with Maria Martin receiving the
Robert F. Kennedy Journalism Award, 2000.

Thus, Sister Dianna, in our interactions, inspired me to continue exploring the human condition. As a journalist who aims to arrive at the truth, I finally gained her trust.

> *With the eyes of a hawk, I watched you. I digested your words and observed your actions, Maria, through your gentleness and non-intrusive manner, you lured me out of my shell—unconsciously giving me the courage to risk trusting again. You helped me to see goodness. Maria, you were that goodness. I saw in you a woman of dignity and conviction—a woman of compassion and of hope—a colorful strand of goodness that has given me and many (other) survivors a renewed trust in the human family. Thank you for this rare gift.*

I will forever be grateful to Sister Dianna, for having allowed me to tell a part of her story. I am glad to report that Ortiz's memory slowly returned. As result, with Patricia Davis, she wrote *The Blindfold's Eye: My Journey from Torture to Truth*, a powerful memoir published in 2002. She also went on to become an outspoken human rights activist and advocate for victims of torture worldwide, founding the Torture Abolition and Survivors Support Coalition International based in Washington, D.C.

Chapter 13

CONNECTING WITH LATIN AMERICAN JOURNALISTS

MY EXPERIENCES DURING MY TENURE at *Latino USA* veered from sublime and satisfying to problematic and painful. Still, my eagerness to have greater Latin American coverage on the program was always present, especially after the awards honoring my specials on Sister Dianna Ortiz.

❖

At the beginning of the twenty-first century, at an especially difficult juncture at Latino USA, I remember a phone call I received during my fellowship from my friend and colleague Mandalit del Barco. Mandalit, based with NPR in Los Angeles was calling with a request, asking for a letter of recommendation. "Maria, I want to apply for Fulbright and Knight fellowships to go to Peru." Even though I was on a deadline writing a twenty-page paper for my international media class, I replied. "Of course, Mandalit. Just give me a deadline."

I thought to myself, "What a great idea," as I wrote Mandalit a strong letter of recommendation. This was a timely request as I had long wanted to expand our Latin American coverage, with reporters and commentators from the region.

Sometime later, after earning my Master's and returning as executive producer of *Latino USA*, I realized, that while I dearly loved the program

I'd created, the office dysfunction and behind-the-scenes backstabbing continued to tear at my soul. I needed new inspiration.

Thus, one day, I dug up that paper I'd written for my class on international media, *Radio and Guatemala's Maya Majority: Cultural Activism and Gaining Access*, which now became the basis for my application for Fulbright and Knight International Press Fellowships. I proposed to spend six months in Guatemala, and six months working with radio stations throughout Central America.

During my Knight interview in Washington, I was asked, "Have you ever thought about going to Uruguay?" I definitely had not. Why the question? It turned out that Knight had a request from the Uruguayan Press Association for a radio trainer. I told the interviewer I would be very happy, if chosen, to work in Uruguay during half my grant period, and the rest of the time in Guatemala.

Thus, a few weeks after the terrible events of September 11, 2001, my trip to Uruguay was underway. I boarded a plane to Montevideo to begin my third act.

❖

In some ways, I was glad to be away and out of the country in the period after 9/11. The reports at the time of censorship in the media, of heightened suspicion of those who appeared Muslim, and the chilling effect in academic circles were frightening.

I experienced this emotional and tragic time in a country I'd never visited, and in a part of Latin America that was new to me, so different in many ways from the Mexico and Central America with which I was familiar. Wandering around the Uruguayan capital of Montevideo, I kept asking myself, "Where are the brown people?"

Sometime later, at a visit to a small history museum in one of the provincial capitals, I saw a small diorama depicting the death in a gunfight of the "last" native Guaraní killed in Uruguay in the early twentieth century. Of course, the truth of this display was debatable. Later, I would learn there were still pockets of Indigenous Uruguayans, as well as a community of Afro-Uruguayans, principally located in the capital. Nonetheless, over 90 percent of Uruguayans were of predominantly European origin, mostly descended from nineteenth- and twentieth-century immigrants whose origin were traced to Spain, Italy, as well as France, Germany, and Britain.

❖

When I arrived in Montevideo, I felt butterflies at the thought of facing the unknown, and at first, a deep-seated lack of self-confidence. While I had a little training experience under my belt, having taught two journalism workshops to radio journalists in Bolivia the previous February, I was still nervous. Then I remembered the saying: "If you want to learn, teach." And, so I took three deep breaths, and prepared myself for the adventure to come.

"I've been here a week now," I wrote to Susan Mills at PBS-TV's *NewsHour*.

> Tomorrow I set out for *el interior* to conduct ethics and radio journalism workshops. It will be interesting to see the countryside and the smaller population centers—over half of Uruguay's population lives in the capital of Montevideo, where the Reverend Sun Yun Moon owns the fanciest mansion (and a newspaper, naturally) . . . and where a prison for political prisoners of the 1970's and 1980's is now an upscale shopping mall. (¡Arriba el Shopping! say the banners).

My training agenda called for me to spend a week doing workshops with journalists in seven different cities of Uruguay. I learned as I went along: preparing like mad for each week-long session, during which I was not only going to share my own experiences and impart skills from the tons of training material I carted, but I also would be learning from every journalist I met.

I loved the names of the places I was to visit: Melo, Durazno, Paysandu, Rivera, Cardona, Salto, Tacuarembó. Driving through the rolling plains and low hills of Uruguay, in my rented car, was like being in an undiscovered wonderland. On the roadside there were only a few billboards, amid small hills and lots of flatlands — as green as Sonoma County in a pre-drought California winter. I drove over bridges crossing river after river, in a dense network of streams and four principal deltas that crisscrossed the country. "*Nunca nos vamos a morir de sed.*" ("Here we will never go thirsty,") boasted Uncas Fernández, my kind host from the Uruguayan Journalists Association.

At each stop along the way I came to appreciate Uruguay's people. I was especially impressed with the committed, funny, and gracious radio journalists and the on-air talent I met in the provincial towns of the Uruguayan countryside. Live radio in Uruguay, where the medium has a long and storied history, is nothing short of an art. In fact, transmissions that spread popular opera from the capital city of Montevideo began in 1920, shortly after Guglielmo Marconi's first broadcast. By October 1, 1922, a soccer game was on the air in Uruguay, possibly the first such match broadcast in the world. At the time of my visit, some eight decades after that historic soccer game, radio remained a major source of information and entertainment in this small nation, sandwiched both geographically and historically between its powerful neighbors, Brazil and Argentina.

The country was then at a political crossroads, with the press beginning to again experience freedom of expression for the first time in decades. Now, Uruguay is ranked high among Latin American countries in democracy, peace, absence of corruption, and press freedom. But back in 2002, journalists were still feeling the effects of the country's so-called "dirty war," a period of civil unrest which lasted from 1973 to 1985 during which a military dictatorship had ruled the country. During those years, press freedoms were severely curtailed. Many journalists I met told me of working under an enduring legacy of self-censorship from that era.

At the time of my tour, those working behind radio microphones were masters in the art of live radio. In every Uruguayan town I visited, the character of what we would call "talk" programming never failed to impress me. I was thrilled to wake up early for visits to local stations, where I observed and sometimes participated in morning programs.

For example, in Tacuarembó — a city of 60,000 located in the center of the country — a morning program called *Adelante* on Radio Zorilla was more like a community bulletin board than a talk show. Three or four people might be seated around a small table, in tune with each other and smoothly reading news, taking phone calls, acting out commercials, doing in-studio interviews, and playing music — all produced live and at a fast and rhythmic pace. Neither the radio equipment nor the studio were state-of-the-art, but you wouldn't know that from the animated and engaging sounds coming out of the radio.

It may not have sounded that much different from many of our own morning shows, but believe me, the content and the spirit of the programming was quite distinct from that of the shock jocks and one-sided political commentators we had become accustomed to in the U.S. On programs in Uruguay's interior, the pace may have been hectic, but the conversation was warm, friendly, and intelligent. On programs such as *Adelante* there was humor, but not put-downs. And though these were commercial stations, shows featured a huge element of public service. People dropped in and were invited to tell their stories. One morning, for instance, a young man described his recently stolen bicycle and let people know how they could reach him if his only mode of transportation were sighted. An older woman told potential employers in the listening audience about her job skills. This was followed by a commercial break, the news, and fast-paced, witty conversation spiced with family-friendly jokes and Uruguayan colloquialisms.

Radio veteran Ovidio Ramon Silva, who headed up the *Adelante* team of four announcers and who'd worked in radio for forty years, told me:

> What's unique about radio in Uruguay, and particularly in the provinces, is that, more than entertainment, the medium is a community service. Our style of radio is extremely participatory, agile, and spontaneous. Our people are

permanently tuned into the radio and consider it a possible solution to the community's problems. They see a (radio) program as a social remedy, a place where they can obtain information and perhaps solutions.

This philosophy about the role of radio in a community has always resonated with me. It was this aspect of the media, and the journalists I encountered — in a country I didn't even know I'd enjoy visiting — that so impressed me. In part because of this, Uruguay's lively spirit remains vividly with me many years later.

Chapter 14

GUATEMALA'S INDIGENOUS PEOPLES PURSUE VOICE, MEET RESISTANCE

THEY'RE LOCATED IN THE SMALLEST communities — tiny *aldeas* not reached by newspapers, or even television. Some are found in humble homes, next to patios where Indigenous women sit on the ground weaving intricate patterns on back-strap looms. Others are in tiny *tiendas*, the closet-size neighborhood stores selling everything from a single cigarette or envelope to a bottle of soda pop.

The only way you know these locations house the local radio station is by the tell-tale antennas reaching up out of metal or stucco roofs to the Guatemalan skies. When I arrived in 2002 to this land of "eternal spring/eternal tyranny," as writer Jean Marie Simon calls Guatemala, community radio was being birthed in this tragic and beautiful land born of the hopes raised by the peace accords that ended the continent's then longest civil war in 1996.

Much of the burden of the violence of that bloody, armed conflict that took 200,000 Guatemalan lives, fell on the Indigenous people in the rural areas, who make up about half of the country's population. The peace accords had opened the door to the hope that Guatemala's Indigenous majority, marginalized for more than 500 years, might someday enjoy the promise of a "multiethnic, multilingual society."

The country's Maya population, who make up some twenty-two different language groups, and the black Garifuna population of the

Atlantic coast, hoped the peace agreements would usher in an era of greater access to the media. They dreamed especially of one that would reach their communities in their own languages. Some twenty years later, many of these hopes for a more democratic country have fallen short. There have been a series of corrupt governments, with ties to narco traffickers and mafias. At times, it seems the country is returning to the days of death squad violence.

For a while, it appeared as if in the area of radio, there was still hope for democratic initiatives. At first, evangelicals and former guerrillas came together to try to create *radios comunitarias*—a system of local, community-run radio stations that would, in the words of El Salvador's martyred Archbishop Arnulfo Romero, "give voice to the voiceless." For years, hundreds of these community radio advocates traveled to the capital from villages throughout the country, riding many hours on crowded buses to ask the government in Guatemala City to recognize their community radio stations.

Some two decades later, most of these stations are still illegal under Guatemala's current telecommunications law, and efforts to pass a proposed "Law on Community Media and Mass Communication" have fallen short. This bill would've reserved certain radio frequencies on national, regional and local levels for the use of "Associations and Community Councils, at the service of the community." While proponents say that allowing local people and civil society groups to run community radio stations would strengthen local identity and democracy and help the country work toward a culture of peace, commercial broadcasters have generally opposed the idea. Spokespersons for the *Cámara de Difusión*—the Chamber of Broadcasters—say the proposed law would create confusion and competition in the already existing "legal" broadcast system.

I was present when then *Cámara* President Roberto Boccatelli spoke at a meeting of lawmakers and representatives of community radio organizations in Guatemala City. He said, "*No porque yo soy indígena que me van a dar todo porque soy el rey del pueblo*—just because I'm Indigenous doesn't mean I should get it all as if I were King." I found the statement both interesting and ironic, given that his words came shortly after Guatemala had signed peace accords, and when so few of the promises made to expand the rights to a people so long marginalized and discriminated against have not been kept.

More than two decades of experience in U.S. Latino community/public radio, have shown me enough not to be surprised at the resistance to changes in the status quo. Thirty years after the first Latino owned and operated community radio station went on the air in this country (KBBF-FM in Santa Rosa, California) for instance, there were still no Latino editors at National Public Radio.

In Guatemala meanwhile, the struggle for a more inclusive media continues. As this process goes on, so do government auctions to sell off remaining frequencies to the highest bidder, further blocking the possibilities of many community radio stations from becoming part of the established media in Guatemala — the home to which I always returned.

Chapter 15

FROM LATIN AMERICA TO *LATINO USA*

I CAME BACK FROM my year in Uruguay and Guatemala to a country mired in post-9/11 fear and suspicion. Every day, the administration of President George W. Bush made proclamations of war.

In a new millennium, change of all kinds was upon us, and demographic shifts were dramatic. The 2000 U.S. Census, used the term "Latino" for the first time as well as "Hispanic," and had determined there were then more than thirty-five million Hispanics in the U.S., with rapid growth predicted. By 2050, according to demographic data, one-third of the U.S. population would be Latino.

By 2003, *Latino USA* had been on the air for ten years. We had beaten the odds and defied the naysayers, including those who had told us that Latinos only listened to programs in Spanish. They had refused to see that there are *three* Latino audiences — monolingual Spanish and monolingual English-speakers, and bilingual audiences. *Latino USA* had appealed to two of those publics, bringing new listeners to expand the traditionally white and aging audience for public radio. However, after a successful decade of service, *Latino USA* was running out of money. By all indications, the station that housed it had lost interest in supporting it.

On my return, keeping the project alive was a priority, and one of these efforts involved a discussion with NPR, in which I tried to convince them to make a greater investment in the show. I feared the system would resort to their old argument of "Latino programs don't work on public radio; you have to mainstream this content." This was an argument that NPR had made ten years earlier and we have proved them wrong. Yet, at the time, public radio had still failed to "mainstream" Latino issues in their content.

While still on leave, in September 2002, I attended the Latino Radio Summit, held in Sonoma County, California, home of KBBF, the nation's first Latino-controlled public radio station and my first radio home. Conference organizers wanted to examine the gains Latinos had made in the preceding three decades. The meeting was a reunion of Latino broadcasters, independent producers, and other players in the system, for the purpose of discussing the future of public radio and its importance to Latinos in the U.S. and Puerto Rico. According to Latino Summit Planning Committee member Hugo Morales, executive director of the Radio Bilingüe Latino Radio Network, one of the major challenges was "how we extend our services to Latinos living in urban areas." Morales confirmed that most of the attending stations "broadcast *Latino USA*."

During the Summit, I strategized ways to keep *Latino USA* viable. I proposed to have NPR make a greater investment in the program, and transition the production from Austin to its then new Los Angeles Bureau. NPR representatives at the Summit didn't seem to support my argument. When I made the same case for this "NPR transition," to the Corporation for Public Broadcasting (CPB), I was told the proposal was "premature." Still, CPB appeared interested in some kind of funding for *Latino USA*, especially in the area of training. Thus, I pitched them a project that I had been thinking about, even researching for a while, a project that reported on Central America's post-war situation. I framed it as a training project: an ambitious bilingual documentary series, each segment reported by teams made up of veteran radio journalists experienced in Latin American reporting, an early-career reporter/producer from one of the Latino-controlled stations or an independent public radio producer, as well a Central American reporter. The proposal appealed to me for a great number of reasons: the Central American connection of course was one. While the census data indicated that the fastest growing segment of the

U.S. Latino population consisted of Central Americans, there was precious little coverage of the region, now that it was generally at peace and the news crews covering its civil conflicts had decamped to other hot spots.

With our impending financial crisis, keeping the program alive was a priority. In that quest, I asked the CPB representatives. "You have a rolling deadline, right?" "Oh no, that's changed now," they replied. They mentioned a deadline that was less than a week away. Gulp! Given the red tape at the University of Texas, there was no way a grant could be written and navigated through UT's bureaucracy in a week. I got to thinking—since I was technically still on leave from Latino USA, I was at the time considered an "independent producer" in the public radio system. Then, I inquired, "Can I apply as an independent producer?" CPB responded. "You can apply as anything you like just so you make the deadline."

With that information, the next day I contacted grant writer Holly VanScoy, who was helping *Latino USA* with fundraising. VanScoy and I worked non-stop for four days with only a few hours of sleep each night as we cranked out what I thought was a rockin' proposal that called for:

> *A comprehensive, twenty-six-part bilingual reporting project from and about the condition of Central America and Central Americans some two decades after the civil strife that tore apart many countries in the region.*

> *The overarching goal of the effort is to attract new English- and Spanish-speaking listeners to public radio, while delivering in-depth, balanced content about Central America that engages and informs public radio's current audiences. A parallel goal is to foster and support the development of mid-career public radio producers, by enhancing their understanding of Central America, connecting them to news and information sources in Central American nations, and providing them with opportunities to collaborate with experienced, senior producers to create memorable programming for their audiences.*

> A third important goal is leveraging the existing resources
> of project partner to build production capacity and extend
> audience reach . . . including but not limited to Latino USA, NPR,
> Radio Bilingüe, independent producer, Latino-controlled radio
> stations in the U.S., community radio stations, and journalists in
> Central America.

We made the deadline.

Several months later we learned we had been awarded $300,000 dollars for the reporting project *Despues de la Guerras: Central America After the Wars.* Nonetheless, my attempt to serve *Latino USA* backfired on me. This effort was ultimately used to oust me from the project I had created.

As I look back at this chapter of my life, I can't help but also think about connections these events have with the work I've been doing with Latin American journalists. They tell horrible stories, of harassment and persecution — nothing like what happened to me. These journalists suffer, daily, a lashing out by an entrenched power structure that refuses to depart from the old ways of corruption, and undemocratic practices. But I do see an analogy. In *this* country, there are and have been sectors that cling to the way things have always been. They do what they can to resist change when their world is challenged. This happens from boardrooms to police stations to universities to media entities throughout our country. Public radio had been slower and more resistant to change than even other media. This had been detrimental to society as well as to the institution of public broadcasting.

I offer that if public media had been quicker, not as resistant to respond to this country's demographic changes, perhaps the chasm we are now seeing in our society wouldn't be as great. Perhaps, there would be greater understanding and less of the backlash we are confronting along racial, ethnic, and economic lines in this country.

Martin in Oaxaca with the late NPR commentator and author Vertamae Grosvenor.

Chapter 16

■ ● ■ ■ ■ ♦ ● ■ ■ ● ■

DESPUES DE LAS GUERRAS AND TRAINING JOURNALISTS

IT WAS MY BELIEF that the reporting project, *Después de las Guerras: Central America After the Wars* would help to create greater understanding between people — in this case, between those from north and south in the Western Hemisphere. This was my essential goal, despite the difficulties the project had created for me. So, after everything ended at *Latino USA*, I prepared to again cross borders. This time I would be traveling back to Guatemala to establish a base to report and executive-produce a project involving some two-dozen reporters, from Central America and the United States.

In my desire to fashion greater cross-cultural understanding, I'd left National Public Radio to start *Latino USA* in the early 1990s. Now, it was my aim to create a memorable, well-produced series that would give listeners reasons to understand what had been going on in Central America since the wars ended. After the violence diminished, except when an occasional hurricane struck, the mainstream media had not regularly reported on this region.

I wanted audiences, those fluent in Spanish as well as English, to understand the social, economic, and historical connection between the U.S. and the nations often known as "banana republics." I wanted to use every radio journalism skill I had gained, and the talents of an amazing cadre of veteran and new reporters and producers, to tell the untold stories of the region.

As I said, while I admire the work of those who produce the artful documentary, I have always perceived a greater need for radio to play a substantive role in bridging cultures and creating understanding through fair, accurate, and inclusive information. Still, the kind of radio I aim to produce is not only about mission but craft. It's not enough to produce programs that people "should" listen to. On the contrary, I hope the radio I make is also something audiences "want" to hear. If producing radio that touches people's hearts and minds has been one of my guiding production values over the last four decades, the other is my desire to "hook them in!" I make every attempt to win over listeners with compelling sound, inspired pacing, vivid writing, and informed editing.

The sounds of the communities I cover often motivate and guide creative production. Appropriate music, cadences of speech, the different accents of my subjects — whether speaking English, Spanish, or an Indigenous language — can all add another dimension to a story, a new layer of richness to a production.

Voice-over translations pose an opportunity for creating lovely sound montages, with one language weaving in and out of the other. In addition, how one treats voice-overs and uses original interviews can validate the humanity of one's sources.

For instance, when I'm working with a Spanish-language interview, I strive to establish what a person is saying first, to let him or her express a complete thought before bringing in the English-language voice-over. Establishing a complete thought may take ten or twelve seconds — perhaps even longer — but in that process, one validates the dignity of the person whose voice is part of the production and whose story I'm telling. By allowing non-English languages to breathe, we show respect for the increasing number of Americans who speak Spanish and other languages, and who — more each day — are becoming part of our audiences. To keep the production interesting, I'll also sometimes alternate between voice-overs and paraphrases, even in the same interview.

I used all of these techniques in *Después de las Guerras*, which aired in twelve parts during 2004 and 2005. One segment, for example, explores the issue of Indigenous identity. A main character is a fifteen-year-old young Maya woman named Casimira Xiloj Herrera, who made the decision to break away from her mother's and grandmother's tradition of wearing Indigenous clothing, called *traje*. In one scene, I created a trilingual production—as Casimira spoke to her Quiché Maya speaking-grandmother through her mother, who translated from Spanish to Quiché Maya.

In another piece from the series, *Santa Maria: A Tale of One Village*, I recounted the story of just one of the hundreds of Guatemalan communities that experienced massacres. I used voice-overs for a massacre survivor, Edwin, and his father, Manuel Canil. Edwin's story is so poignant and powerful that I attempted to weave the two languages together in such a way as to have much of the original version heard directly, or "in the clear." I think the authentic emotion comes through even for those who don't speak Spanish. At the same time, the voice that translates Edwin's story has a powerful quality of its own, which I believe enhances the entire scene. The transcript from that segment follows:

> EDWIN: *Hay veces que se me dificulta, pero si hay veces que si puedo . . . [Edwin's voice fades for my paraphrase.]*

> NARRATION: *Edwin Canil says it's hard for him to talk about the events of February, 1982 . . . In the United States then, Ronald Reagan was president . . . The headlines in U.S. newspapers told of other happenings in Central America, in El Salvador and Nicaragua, but there was little news of what was taking place in this part of the region—about how, just south of the Mexican border, a column of Guatemalan soldiers marched into the isolated jungle settlement called Santa María Tzejá. Edwin was just six years old then . . .*

EDWIN: [We hear Edwin telling his story, as the Spanish rolls untranslated, for fifteen seconds.] Solo recuerdo que salí corriendo me metí entre la vegetación.... El ejército con toda su carga, y yo no puedo pasar entre eso... y [sighs]... y no me fui muy lejos... [Spanish fades, voice-over comes in.]

ENGLISH VOICE-OVER: I only remember running... When I heard the gun shots and screams, I didn't turn around [Spanish very audible under this]... There was a fallen tree trunk, and there I hid. Then I heard a little girl crying, and it was my little sister... [pause]. It seemed as if I were watching a play. Then, I saw a soldier lift her up and take out his knife... and... [pause] EDWIN: [Voice comes up]... y cuando vi un soldado... agarró y levantó a mi hermanita... sacó su cuchillo... [Edwin becomes more emotional, he pauses, chokes up. We hear this for six to seven seconds.]

ENGLISH VOICE-OVER CONTINUES: He took her arm and cut it off, and threw it away... I did not understand what I was seeing, I did not know what death was... [long pause]. Later, when the soldiers left [sobs in background], I went back to where the bodies lay in a circle, and I laid down with them, waiting for them to wake up—my mother, my grandmother, my cousins and uncles... my little sister... I began to talk to them: "Mother. Grandmother." They would not answer, they wouldn't wake up.

EDWIN: [Voice comes up]... Nadie se levanta, nadie... y vi a mi hermanita—lo que yo recuerdo. Vi a mi hermanita, ya no tenía cabeza, se despedazó todo...

ENGLISH VOICE-OVER: Then I saw my little sister, without her head... My mother, with a bullet... I was afraid, I was scared for the first time. Then I left... [sniffs]

EDWIN: [Voice comes up] . . . *Fue la primera vez que sentí miedo, y salí* . . . It was the first time I felt fear, and I left.

I "auditioned" various voices for the role of Edwin. For the voice of the father, the amazing survivor Manuel Canil, I knew that the voice of the late maestro and Xic-Indio (Chicano/Indian) poet Raul Salinas would not only be great for radio but would also reflect the spirit of Manuel — two voices from different continents with somewhat related life experiences, coming together through documentary production to tell a powerful tale. These creative endeavors sometimes felt as if they called for more than I could give, but they came with the daring of desire to create access and tell stories.

Chapter 17

ONCE AGAIN, STARTING OVER

THESE PRODUCTIONS WERE not only challenging, but the post-production was also problematic. It took many months to convince the administration at KUT Radio in Austin to air the finished series air on *Latino USA*. Even though at times I would convince myself that the door that had closed in my old project might signal a window opening to new opportunities, it was hard not to feel wounded. "Why am I having to start everything from scratch again?" I asked myself repeatedly. "Why am I once again building a new project infrastructure by myself? Haven't I spent the better part of the last twelve years doing that?"

For the first few months after I returned to Guatemala to execute the project, I felt almost paralyzed by the challenges of hiring staff, setting up a production schedule, making travel arrangements and editorial decisions; not to mention having to continue raising funds, since my CPB grant only parsed out partial payment until matching funds could be raised from other sources.

❖

So, when I arrived in Guatemala to finally start production, I was still mired in feeling sorry for what I perceived as the injustice that had happened. But, then I picked up a book of writings by the Zapatista leader Subcomandante Marcos — it was the beginning of 2004, the tenth anniversary of the Zapatista Army of National Liberation's uprising in Chiapas, Mexico, an event we had covered extensively when I was at *Latino USA*. Reading about the plight of Mexico's Indigenous people allowed me to see the injustice I had suffered from a fresh perspective. "Hello, Maria!" I told myself. "There is *perceived injustice* and then there is *tangible injustice* that's been such a central part of a culture for hundreds of years that some felt needed an armed revolution to change." I was pulled to Chiapas, to see what was going on with the Zapatista story for myself.

Still feeling de-energized, I took the bus from Antigua to Guatemala City, from there to the border town of Tecun Uman, and then into Mexico and north to San Cristobal de las Casas, Chiapas. From that regional capital—where as late as the 1960s Indigenous people were not even allowed to walk on city sidewalks—I visited Zapatista-sympathetic communities, witnessing the poverty and marginalization that had led to an armed insurrection ten years earlier. This took place as the North American Free Trade Agreement (NAFTA) was beginning to be implemented. Mexican politicians were touting the trade deal as one that would make Mexico a "first world" country. The Zapatista uprising, and the subsequent military occupation of Chiapas, showed how far this was from happening.

This reporting trip allowed me to hear other untold stories. It pulled me out of my depression, giving me the inspiration to continue my work. Two years later, my series of twenty-four thirty-minute episodes (twelve each in Spanish and English) was completed. I was pleased that it aired on over 100 stations and won a number of awards, although most of the pieces were not accepted for airing on NPR.

❖

Because it was hard for me to sell my reporting about Central America to public radio, I decided to continue my work training local journalists in Guatemala and Central America. I also was invited to Bolivia on a number of occasions to work with mostly rural Indigenous journalists.

These experiences changed my life.

While working for public radio in the U.S., I'd often felt that I didn't get enough credit or thanks for what I did. But, when I completed each training session in Guatemala or in Bolivia, the gratitude was so effusive, it was almost embarrassing. Working with these journalists took me back to my days at bilingual radio station KBBF, to a time when it was so apparent that for many communities, radio was a lifeline and not a luxury.

It's not surprising, for instance, that some of the first battles for media democratization in Guatemala since the signing of peace accords in the mid-1990s are still being fought over for control of radio frequencies. Or, that in Bolivia and Venezuela, populist governments trying to create social change set up community radio networks. While television, cable, and the Internet are making inroads throughout the continent, radio remains a powerful mass medium in the region, reaching hills and rural areas away from the cities where other media cannot reach.

Yes, radio in places like Guatemala, Bolivia, and Uruguay is truly a people's medium. In working with many journalists, I've been greatly impressed with *comunicadores sociales* who possess a strong commitment to serving the public and to helping their listeners become active participants in a peaceful democracy. Such communicators often do their vital work with few resources and with little protection from the law. Often, they risk their lives and livelihoods. Their experiences re-inspired me at a time when I needed to look beyond the politics of public radio and the continued resistance in some quarters to serve a changing audience.

And, so in the last two decades, I've found myself spending more of my time teaching and working with these *periodistas empíricos* — journalists with no formal training — where I share my experiences and learn from theirs, while recalling a time when I, too, had little formal training but a great deal of commitment to telling stories that would make a difference and, just maybe, a better world.

Training Radio Journalists in Guatemala.

Chapter 18

FROM RADIO GUATE TO GUATEDIGITAL

AS I'VE CONTINUED training rural and provincial journalists, especially in Guatemala, their vulnerability has become very clear. In a country only two decades out of a long civil war, these are the journalists with the least formal training who were most subject to threats and attacks — especially when reporting on sensitive issues such as corruption and drug trafficking. These are the reporters who, with little support or resources, provide information to the bulk of Guatemala's seventeen million people. In small communities, these journalists are often caught between a rock and a hard place — reporting news about local officials who may be close to them or their families, or about people who hold extreme power that too often is connected to the larger mafias that, according to many observer and international organizations, now effectively run the country.

Often I wondered how to help these journalists beyond one-shot training workshops. How to help them help themselves? During group exercises these individuals often listed "lack of unity" as one of their greatest challenges. They told me they felt disconnected from other journalists around the country, especially from those who were part of mass media based in the capital. They spoke about being looked down upon by these big-city journalists when they'd come to the provinces, usually to report on some tragedy like a lynching or one of the many natural disasters that plague Guatemala.

I spoke about this dilemma with the staff of the Knight Center for Journalism in the Americas based at the University of Texas at Austin. The Knight Center's mission focuses on helping journalists create and strengthen organizations to elevate professional standards and defend press freedom. Its director, Rosental Alves suggested that these Guatemalan rural journalists become part of an electronic network. Soon after, the journalists themselves agreed, and became connected on an electronic list-serve called *RadioGuate*.

When I began to work with them, few of these journalists had basic digital skills, or even e-mail. With the Knight Center's help, we brought nearly fifty of these journalists together in Guatemala City in August 2005 for the first *Encuentro Internacional Entre Periodistas de los Departamentos y de la Capital de Guatemala* (International Encounter between Guatemalan Journalists from the Capital and the Departments [Provinces]). It was, I believe, an historic occasion, one that began to bridge the gap that existed between rural and provincial journalists and their more educated and elite urban counterparts.

Three years later, after I'd completed my Central American series and returned from a Knight Fellowship for Professional Journalists at Stanford University, I applied for another Knight Fellowship. This called for me to continue the work of training and bringing rural journalists together to help build a digital platform to share stories.

During the course of this particular fellowship, the RadioGuate journalists moved to change their network's name to "GuateDigital." It better reflected the growing diversity of their membership—especially from recently launched cable TV outlets—that I call the "new community media"—and those immersed in the digital age. Soon, they formed a strategic partnership with the digital platform called NoticiasDeMiGente.com (NewsofMyPeople.com), which was devoted to publishing stories of interest to Guatemalan communities within and outside the country. Unfortunately, this last project was not successful for many reasons, including the social gap that existed between the elite techies who created and administered the platform in Guatemala City, and the rural and Indigenous journalists who provided the content.

Maria Martin with Indigenous Women journalists:
Coban, Guatemala 2008.

Still, I remember with pride the second *Encuentro* held outside Guatemala City for three days in late July of 2008. This national gathering brought together these journalists to reflect on this new era of digital journalism opening up to them . . . and it gave them a taste of the democratic possibilities that digital journalism offered. With the help of international trainers — including Christian Espinoza of Cobertura Digital in Ecuador; Peruvian journalist Luz Helguero; and Carlos Dada, the award-winning founder of El Salvador's groundbreaking independent digital newspaper *El Faro* — about fifty participants learned to plan and prepare multimedia reports for existing publications, to create blogs, and to edit video and audio for multimedia packages.

You could see the worlds of these journalists change. Now they could control the product they were producing, with their own words and images, free of censorship. Excited by these new digital skills, Alan Muchuch Cumez of San Juan Comalapa said he was glad to have "learned technological tools and professional techniques that dignified the creativity in journalism and in Guatemala's democracy."

A member of GuateDigital's first governing board, Gladys Morales of Quetzaltenango, expressed that the *Encuentro* would not only strengthen the network of journalists, but would also "help journalists from the interior and the capital to participate more actively in digital journalism and to strengthen their networks for training, solidarity, and support." She added: "We really want to make the most of this great opportunity and to see *GuateDigital* . . . become a great network and provider of information."

As a reminder of the difficulties facing these journalists on a daily basis, Coban-based journalist Angel Martin Tax received a call on the event's last day telling him that his colleague, Eduardo Maaz Bol, had suffered a gun attack when nine bullets were fired into his home and car. Maaz Bol's family narrowly escaped injury. Ironically, this news came just as Tax participated in a panel regarding safety for journalists. Hector Cordero, a journalist from the province of Quiche, pleaded with the head of the Guatemalan Journalists Association and a representative of the human rights prosecutor's office to pay more attention to the plight of journalists in the departments and rural areas of Guatemala. "We are totally helpless," Cordero asserted. "We feel abandoned." My hope had been that as result of the networking and the new digital skills journalists took home from the *Encuentro*, "they were now better equipped with new tools and contacts to fight their isolation."

While there's no doubt that the journalists with whom I've worked have gained much from entering the digital world, the dangers remain. One of many examples is that of the journalist who asked for help from the Guatemalan Journalists Association and the Human Rights Office. To elaborate on what journalists experience, I wrote the following essay in 2009 regarding Hector Cordero's situation, which was published in an academic journal:

> The e-mails come every once in a while. Sometimes the situation they describe is worse than others. This last one had one word written in the subject line: Preocupado–"Worried." My throat tightens. I begin shifting my weight on the cheap blue plastic chair I sit at in this wooden shack of an Internet café in a placid lakeside village in Guatemala. It makes me feel unsettled physically and emotionally.
>
> With that one word, I am transported from the Guatemala where twenty-first century hippies in blonde dreadlocks come to find crystal healers and Reiki masters–drawn by the ethereal beauty of volcanoes, lakes, and esoteric Maya culture–to another Guatemala–one rarely visited by tourists, forgotten by government and until recently, by the major media. I am spirited to a Guatemala where nothing much has really changed since the long war here ended more than a decade ago. There, the violence continues, impunity reigns, and the decisions are still made by men with guns.
>
> The e-mail comes from that other Guatemala. The author is Hector, a thirty-eight-year old television journalist living in the

province of Quiche. Geographically, it's not really that far from here. Hector is a strong man, almost stoic, and would not try to worry anyone needlessly.

Quiche, or El Quiche, as some call it, is one of Guatemala's twenty-two "departments"—equivalent to states in the U.S., or provinces in some other countries. Most of Quiche's people are Indigenous Maya, speaking Quiche, Uspantek, Poq'omchi, and a smattering of other Mayan dialects. During the counter-insurgency campaigns of the war in the eighties, the government regarded the Mayas as easy recruits for the guerrilla rebels. As a result, this department saw some of the bloodiest episodes during Guatemala's long civil war—countless massacres and villages razed to the ground. I remember what my friend Rosa told me about being stationed there with her husband when he was a policeman during the war years—she shivers when she recalls living there—not being able to leave her house in the mornings after hearing screams that went on through the night—afraid of what she might see in the light of day. Inez, who owns a hotel in the town of Chichicastenango, tells me she organized a contingent of people from her town to go into the countryside each morning to look for and bury dead bodies during those years—they always found them, in that other Guatemala.

I've been living in Guatemala, working mostly as a journalism trainer, for almost eight years. I go back and forth to the United States, and had been away for almost a year when I saw Hector for the first time since he was a participant in a series of journalism training courses I conducted.

"Tell me what's been happening in your life," I asked. "Ay, Maria," He just shook his head. "Tanto, tanto." ("So much, so much.")

He had moved beyond reporting for a small family-owned local cable station: his stories now reached the entire country, even the world via the Internet. With his new job for a national TV channel, Hector was able to travel to tiny aldeas in the far-flung nooks and crannies of his province. His voice cracked when he spoke about witnessing extreme poverty and hunger made worse by a drought drying up corn and bean fields. Guatemala has the highest level of chronic malnutrition in Latin America, the fourth highest in the world. "But the worse thing," he said, "are the corrupt politicians—they steal from the people and make the famine and hunger worse." He couldn't hide his anger. He looked a lot older than I remembered.

He told me about politicians who didn't like his questions, and who let him know so. "But then I remembered what you taught me, Maria . . . to ask what the people would want to know."

He also told me about the attempts to bribe him, and when these failed, the threats that followed. The congressman representing his region offered one thousand quetzales (about $120) a month to journalists in Quiche who would only write favorable stories about him. That's a sizeable amount in Guatemala. Hector refused. He had a visit from the congressman's representative—"For you, Cordero, three thousand quetzales." Hector again refused. He hears from several quarters that the congressman is none too happy with him. "Watch out," they warn him.

Now, almost six months later, the evidence of corruption against the congressman is too telling to ignore. Teachers in the region are complaining that in order to keep their jobs, they are being forced to pay the congressman's relatives three thousand quetzales—the equivalent of almost two month's salary. Hector airs the report. The threats become more frequent: "You'll get yours, son of a bitch. We will get you and your family where it hurts."

Today he told me a pickup truck rode alongside his jeep, and a man waved a gun at him. The pickup veered away when they passed a patrol car.

Hector has a nine-year old daughter; his wife is eight months pregnant. The precepts in those training sessions where I taught about the practice of an independent journalism in the public interest, about freedom of expression and the public's right to know, seem hollow and naïve in the face of this violent reality . . . in this more real Guatemala far removed from that seen by day tourists off the cruise ships who spend their time viewing the colonial ruins of Antigua or traveling to ancient Maya pyramids.

This country has one of the highest murder rates in the Americas. Only two percent of murderers are ever brought to trial. In this atmosphere—in this other Guatemala that can pop up anytime, anywhere—there are limits to a free press. And just as I teach about a journalist's social responsibility, each day I ask myself more and more what mine is to journalists like Hector—to ensure that they tell the stories that need to be told and make a difference in their communities, but most of all, that they stay alive.

❖

It was the week after election day in Guatemala. Hector received telephone threats throughout the hard-fought electoral season, especially after the first-round voting, when some mayors in his province lost their posts. They blamed their loss on Hector, not on their own malfeasance and corruption, which Hector's reports had brought to light.

On the night of the election, Hector was driving home with his cameraman, Diego Morales. Another car carrying four armed men stopped their vehicle. They turned out to be the bodyguards of congressional representative Mario Rivera. The thugs beat Hector and Diego savagely. Not surprisingly, the local police publicly blamed Hector for the beating. "He used bad language," they said. A local medical association issued a decree saying no crime was committed, as the bruises Hector and Diego suffered will heal within ten days. Hector's editor went on national television to say this now opens the doors for attacks on journalists everywhere in the country. This is the <u>other</u> Guatemala, where there is a nominal democracy, with elections held and certified, yet corrupt institutions have not changed. And journalists are constantly at risk.

In 2018, it was a shock to learn that Nicaraguan journalist Ángel Gaona had been shot dead while Facebook livestreaming an anti-government protest in the Atlantic-coast city of Bluefields. Gaona had been one of my students at a training workshop six years earlier — and now he was the fifth journalist I personally worked with to be killed as a result of his work.

I often think U.S. journalists do not always appreciate the conditions of privilege we have in this country — even given the challenges. The solidarity I feel with journalists who work under the demanding circumstances of the Latin American media landscape is perhaps one of the reasons I've made Latin America home.

Chapter 19

WHY I LIVE IN GUATEMALA

MY FRIEND, THE TIRELESS Los Angeles journalist Diana Martínez, once asked me to write about why I decided to live in Guatemala — a place I've called home for more than a decade and a half. In many ways, Guatemala chose *me*. Let tell you why I live in Guatemala.

I live in Guatemala because each day I wake up and see the volcano called Agua out my window. As the day goes on, the volcano changes before my eyes. First, it's clear against a blue sky, then the clouds roll in and I only see the top of the cone; then it's totally covered by mist and clouds. By the evening, it may re-appear. It's almost a point of focus for meditation — a lesson in mindfulness as I watch the volcano out of the picture window facing the desk where I work. My computer keeps me in touch with the rest of the world. Agua brings me back to the here and now.

I first visited this Central American country in 1975, and fell in love. Guatemala is one of the loveliest places I've seen. Within its borders are pristine rainforest, monumental ancient Maya cities, and what Aldous Huxley called the most beautiful lake in the world — the majestic and mysterious Atitlán. Almost thirty years later, I returned on a Fulbright scholarship to work with Indigenous radio stations. When it was time to leave, I simply couldn't do it.

Somehow, Guatemala feels like home to me. Home is where I've found balance and a healing sanctuary. Home is where it's okay not to do anything at all every once in a while. Home is where I often go to sleep by eight in the evening—something absolutely unheard of in my former life.

In my former life I worked twelve-plus-hour days. In my former life I was "important." In my former life I was my work. Here I'm the person who lives and works and meditates and sometimes tries to write and no one really knows about it. And, that's just fine.

In this life a simple morning greeting from Don Santos the gardener brings a golden light of joy lasting the whole day. An exchange at the laundry or at the corner store can be an exquisitely sweet encounter.

Not everything in Guatemala is sweet, of course. The European Union has characterized it as "one of the most violent countries in the world." And, if you take a look at the State Department's Consular Report on Guatemala, it may make you run for your life: "Violent criminal activity has been a problem in all parts of Guatemala for years, including murder, rape, and armed assaults against foreigners." This is how the report starts, and it gets more frightening as details emerge.

One of these details is that Guatemala is a developing country attempting to rise from one of the longest civil wars in the Hemisphere—more than four decades of conflict that ran from 1954—when the United States helped overthrow the democratically-elected government of Jacobo Arbenz—to 1996, when peace accords ended the ensuing bloody war that killed over 200,000 Guatemalans.

Some twenty years after the official end of this war, the country is still awash with guns. Unemployment and underemployment are high, the birth rate is exploding, and literacy is low. Successive governments, even in this "new democracy," have been to one extent or another corrupt and have neglected social ills.

In Guatemala, about the size of Tennessee, the reality of poverty, illness, crime and the disparity between the rich and the poor is never far away. In effect, what exists here is a situation much like a great deal of this world. Although I certainly don't like it, living here makes me feel closer to reality . . . more alive, more in tune with the majority of humanity. Viewing poverty on a regular basis, I feel more grateful for what I have.

In the U.S., it's often too easy to believe that our reality is what the rest of the world is like. It's too easy to stay in a cozy cocoon of comfort, materialism, and denial — to forget how lucky and privileged Americans are. Guatemala is to some extent uncomfortable even for those with financial resources. Me? I don't often go out past dark; I almost never take public transportation; I hardly ever drive by myself, and certainly never at night.

There are huge contradictions here. They stare you in the face. You encounter such warm and sweet people, yet there is also much death and violence. The legacy of the war is still present in random street crimes. People get killed for theft of their bicycles and cell phones.

Here, my mobility is limited. Or, more accurately, I limit my mobility. But in the need to make my world smaller, that smaller world is somehow richer. I'm more relaxed. I'm more at home in my home. I'm more attuned to what I need. More, yes, balanced.

"Do you have many friends there?" people ask. Not really, I tell them. My work often takes me to the rural areas outside of Antigua and into the gritty capital of Guatemala City. Still, wherever I am in this country, I feel more human warmth on a day-to-day basis than on an average day in El Norte.

These days, I see many more baby boomer-aged Americans on the streets of Antigua. I think they, too, have discovered the economic advantages of being here. Rents are generally cheaper, as are food prices, and foreigners can usually afford hired help.

My Antigua hideaway — most houses here are located behind high walls and thick wooden gates — was even more appealing after I suffered a health crisis, and needed time and a place to heal. This was one place I could afford to live and not need to take on a full-time job for a while.

Still, for me it's not enough to come to Guatemala for the cheaper living and spring-like climate. In order to truly enjoy all the benefits of being here and to be able to live with the disadvantages, I personally feel I have to give back to Guatemala.

Countless Americans and other internationals are here doing exactly that — working in clinics, establishing non-governmental organizations devoted to reproductive health, literacy, micro-lending, and so on. Or, like me, working with rural and Indigenous journalists. In doing this, I think we take part in the process of trying to establish a different relationship with the people of Guatemala than that which has been the traditional way in Central America for so long: "Here come the gringos to plunder and profit, and off they go somewhere else when a better opportunity opens up."

And, so, even given my position of privilege as an American in Guatemala, I have tried to establish authentic connections with the people whom I've brought into my life. I believe I have become a better human being and have improved as a journalist because of these connections, as I continue to explain to U.S. audiences the Central American reality, and the need so many people in the region feel to leave their countries.

Chapter 20

ROSA OF THE WARMEST HEART

HERE IN GUATEMALA I've found a measure of peace, forgiveness, and a more tranquil life that is in tune with my "core values." While I miss the collective work that went into producing radio journalism at NPR, *Latino USA*, and the Central America documentary series (which allowed me to work again with my ideal production team of Angelica Luevano and Walter Morgan), I certainly don't miss the brutal office politics I encountered in public radio.

I have met wonderful people in Guatemala, including many terrific journalists. Maybe, in some way, living here has brought me back in touch with the Mexico of my childhood and the warm hearts often found in Latin American cultures. Just about the warmest heart I've met belonged to a woman named Rosa Yllescas; she worked for me for ten years and passed away in 2012 when I wrote this remembrance.

> *Rosa came into my life knocking on the door of the home that was temporarily mine in this strange place that life had decided to bring me. She was the first sign I saw of Guatemala's sweetness and pure generosity, despite a life that had not treated her well. She was kind and feisty and took pride in doing a good job—always. Despite having little education, she had innate smarts and a lot of initiative. Often, Rosa wistfully wished she'd had more opportunities to learn.*

It had been ten years since I opened my sublet apartment's door and discovered to my surprise that Rosa came along with it. She wanted to know if I wanted her to cook for me. "Well, okay," I said. "No one's ever cooked for me before." However, since she was part of the rental agreement, I said "sure."

Rosa was funny in her colorful telling of life in the streets of her hometown of Jocotenango. So near Antigua, yet she described those streets as meaner — where violence and death were much closer.

When I decided to leave the apartment where she worked — it felt so far from the "real" Antigua, more like a colonial Disneyland — it only seemed right for her to come along, even though my new place already included someone who cleaned. The more Rosa told me of the woman for whom she worked and whose apartment I had been subletting, the more I wanted to protect her from this seemingly ungrateful boss. Her boss expected Rosa to clean and wash and cook for up to six guests for no extra pay beyond the fifty *quetzales* (about six dollars) per week she paid her. She once told Rosa she was going home to Cuba for Christmas and would leave her the traditional Christmas basket of gifts for employees at the house. When Rosa arrived, she found an empty basket and a note saying that because Rosa was late (sometimes the buses do run late in Guatemala), the woman had decided to take the contents of the basket with her.

Thus, Rosa came with me to my new home located at *El Callejón del Burrito*. I rationalized that she could teach me to cook Guatemalan style. Of course, I never learned. I worked on my computer. Rosa cooked or cleaned. I'd never lived in a neater place.

Sometimes, when I had less work, we organized my closet, or the bathroom shelves, or my ever-growing collections of journalism training materials — all this while watching *novelas* or a movie. When I was sick, she would make me *te de manzanilla* (chamomile tea) or *caldo de pollo* (chicken soup). I loved this.

She'd tell me about her life, and I'd share some stories about mine. Abandoned by her mother at a young age, Rosa was raised by a not-so-gentle grandmother. As a young wife during the war, she had followed her policeman husband to Quiche at the height of the violence. She miscarried several times and lost a little infant girl during those stressful times. She'd describe hearing bullets and screams during the long nights she was left alone, afraid to go out for fear of what she'd find.

Then and later, Rosa found comfort in the church, in *La Virgen*, and in her yearly pilgrimages to venerate the Black Christ of Esquipulas near the Honduran border, never failing to bring me back some kind of holy souvenir. I also brought her gifts from *my* travels — often religious pictures and statues I knew she'd appreciate. These were often sacred objects — from Notre Dame in France, and Russian Orthodox icons from Alaska, for example. I brought her Virgins of Guadalupe from Mexico — although none were as lovely as the large one her husband painted for me when Rosa asked him to do so.

These last years, when I was so busy and she was sick, I'd missed our talks. Rosa had become my mother, my sister, and my friend. All of this wrapped up in the ever-so-complicated relationship between the servant and the served.

On this day, Rosa, as you are laid to rest before the funeral, I see some of my gifts hanging in your kitchen, now transformed into a sacred place where your body lies in state in a coffin of plastic white and gold. Black velvet curtains hang behind you, Rosa, masking the entrance to your cramped bedroom. Now you are surrounded by white angels, burning candles, and a profusion of flowers — white lilies and daisies. You would buy me *flores* every Monday at the market, and you made my home beautiful. Now it's my turn to wander into the labyrinth of the *mercado* and bring some *flores* to you.

You once told me about your daughter, just under two, who had taken ill. There was no money for a taxi or even the bus. You walked to the hospital carrying your small daughter in your arms. They took their time to see the baby . . . and she died. "*Esa niña murió de pobreza*," you told me. "That child died of poverty."

I wonder, dear Rosa, if this was also the case with you. It was clear you did not get the best of care each time you had to go into the National

Hospital in San Felipe. Sometimes they didn't even have a room or a bed for you, and you'd be left on a gurney in the hall, crying in pain. The doctors there had performed three abdominal surgeries on your body during the preceding three years, but it was only after the final operation that they diagnosed intestinal cancer. By then, they said it was too late, that only twenty percent of your intestines were working. "No *auguantó, Rosa*," your husband told me last Tuesday morning. "Her body couldn't take it." But I think: "*Moriste de pobreza*," It was poverty that killed *you*, too.

Yes. I gave you money to help pay the hospital bill. But, I wonder dear Rosa, if there was something more I could've done.

Now, your photographs hang on the wall of my kitchen in Antigua — always a reminder of your vivid presence, your funny stories, your focused work. They also bring to mind all that yet has to be done in Guatemala so that lovely and talented people like you may fulfill their desires for a better life.

Chapter 21

EPILOGUE: LOOKING BACK— 40+ YEARS

IN LATE 2015, the Benson Latin American Library at the University of Texas at Austin, to which I donated my papers, hosted an event commemorating my long life in public radio. It was a lovely experience in many ways, strange in others. It was like having my life pass by before my eyes, as in the Albert Brooks and Meryl Streep film, *Defending Your Life*, in which one has to prove the merit of one's actions before going on to the next astral plane or risk being sent back to Earth to do life over again.

In my own version of this process, and given the testimonials that were provided, I felt as I might have passed. One UT Media account of the event read:

> *"Fearless." "Relentless." "Courageous." "Caring." These are just some of the superlatives that were used to describe Maria Martin, whose forty years as a radio journalist were celebrated in a tribute...*
>
> *Martin's role as a pioneer and mentor cannot be overemphasized, said Mercedes de Uriarte, professor emerita at the UT School of Journalism. Martin's efforts to tell Latino stories were often met with resistance, and sometimes with hostility, in the newsroom. "We owe Maria a debt of gratitude for hanging in there and not giving up," affirmed Uriarte.*

> *Former protégé María Hinojosa, in a video made especially for the occasion, said Martin taught her that journalism is about service and giving. "We mustn't close our eyes to the stories that are right next to us," Martin told her.*
>
> *In a video message recorded for the occasion, Ellin O'Leary, Youth Radio founder, said to Martin: "You are always standing behind democracy whether there is democracy in the country or not."*

It was a gratifying experience to hear these testimonials. At the same time, I wondered what else needed to happen to ensure that my efforts — and those of so many others over the years — would continue to make public radio *truly* public.

A few years ago, the then executive director of the influential Association of Independents in Radio Sue Schardt queried, "Can public radio live up to its name?" Her point reflected what I've been saying and thinking for decades, particularly as she clarified. "Are we here for the eleven percent of the public or for all of it?" She argued that public broadcasting had arrived at a "transformational moment" in which it "must choose whether to let the forces that are coming toward us define what we will become, or to decide on our own terms what path we take." She had reached a conclusion regarding public radio's marketing, programming, and audience-building strategy over the preceding decade: "What happened as a result is that we unwittingly cultivated a core audience that is predominantly white, liberal, highly educated, elite."

For me, this was the same warning I'd been sounding for over thirty years, falling mostly on deaf ears. I hope and pray public media's decision makers have by now heard this message enough, and have seen the tragic consequences of a divided society as a spur to be more diverse and inclusive — in more than just a "token" manner. Nevertheless, the political and social milieu of the past few years makes it abundantly clear that we still have much work to do to heal our broken and alienated United States of America, not to mention our fractured planet.

Sometimes I look back and ask myself what I might have done differently these last forty years. I recognize that I may have been thin-skinned, and perhaps not as strategic as I could've been. I might say now to my younger self: "Don't take things so personally. Surround yourself with allies, with counselors, and with spiritual support and guidance in order not to lose your power." In my view, these strategies would have allowed me to work longer and smarter in engaging the long process of creating change.

Maybe it's just the passage of time that will eventually bring it about. Younger Americans today are much more comfortable with diversity than many of those in my generation and those that came before us. There are more Americans of mixed heritage, like me. As I told those who gathered that day in Austin, "When you are 'caught in the middle,' you are not only placed in a situation of occasional discomfort; but out of that condition often comes opportunities for understanding, to bring sides closer together—to create a space for compassion and restorative justice." I have great hopes that as the number of these bridge builders increases, they can help to create a better, more tolerant society than that which exists today.

Societal transformation is a tough and taxing proposition. I see this every day in Guatemala and other places in Latin America where journalists attempting to exercise their human right to free expression face threats and dangers from an entrenched system that doesn't want the reality of its corruption and greed to come to light. But let us consider the consequences—everywhere—of *not* adapting to new realities. In politics and the media, the questions always has been: Who decides the terms of the dialogue? Who sets the rules for the debate? These questions are even *more* important now than they were in 1967, when public media was born, or in the 1970's, when the civil rights movement grew. The transformations that began then are still works in progress— in education, police community relations, and in the media, both public and commercial. Genuine systemic change is something we need to be committed to for the long term, if we are to build an America — in the sense of a country, continent, and a world that is peaceful and just.

How do we move to a new paradigm that goes beyond creating or adding to existing social tensions and conflict — one that also considers the need for forgiveness and compassion, and the hard truth that when it comes to race and difference, just about all human beings are wounded? While I don't know all the answers to these questions, I offer that we need to continue engaging in a sustained dialogue, which takes these queries into consideration for the long haul, not only in wake of protest and violence. This is where the role of public and other media can be significant at a time when so much of our future is on shaky ground.

❖

In the last few years I've been more active covering Central America. After having had major radio vehicles such as NPR's *Foreign Desk* and even programs like *Latino USA* or *Radio Ambulante* reject my pitches over many years, at least for the moment there's no longer the cyclical disinterest. When Mr. Trump was elected in 2016, it became clear to me that immigration would be an even more pressing issue — presenting stories crying to be told and contexts needing to be explained. Toward that end, I began pitching short news briefs to NPR's *News Desk*, finding open editorial minds this time around. Then I began the arduous process of writing grants to report, travel, and pay my bills so that I could tell stories in an in-depth and comprehensive manner. It was my hypothesis, back in 2016 and 2017, that even the increase in deportations and a harder-line immigration policy wouldn't keep many Central Americans from trying to leave. Violence, economic insecurity, and corruption are all increasing, instead of getting better as these countries became nominal "democracies." The hope for a better future, for Guatemala and most of Central America seems a long way away for most people in this region. Many, seeing little hope for change, are exercising their human right to migrate, voting with their feet to go to a place where they might be able to find conditions for survival and a future for their children. This all the more so, when it's apparent there's now a lack of support from the U.S. for democratization and anti-corruption efforts.

❖

Thus, even given the shortcomings of public broadcasting, it's still a valuable venue that strives to be free from commercial and political pressure, although not always in ideal ways. In my view, an independent public broadcasting system that's robust, diverse, and inclusive must be recognized as a great treasure that can contribute to informing the public and shore up our fragile democracy, as well as to inform on the progress or lack of democratization around the world. The failure of commercial media to be democracy's watchdog and to report fully in the early stages of the 2016 presidential campaign is a glaring example of how commercial media, dedicated to ratings, can fail the democratic process. As I've said — perhaps *ad nauseum* — in order to fulfill its promise, public media must democratize its programs and diversify its personnel in the broadest terms, so as to reflect not only diversity of race, but also of class, age, and gender.

❖

In the meantime, I will continue to make my contributions through public and independent media in the U.S. and Latin America. I will tell stories — in English and Spanish — that touch people's minds and hearts, writing narratives that strive to improve cultural understanding among people.

And while I applaud efforts to broaden audiences through a growing youth/millennial focus, I also smile at the thought that, once again, a lack of vision and failure to be inclusive might be pushing out veteran producers, especially journalists who've been groundbreakers. I've witnessed Native American, Asian, and other minority journalists —

especially women—marginalized at a time in their lives when their experiences could make for great contributions.

As I told that audience at the University of Texas event commemorating four decades of activity in public radio:

> *Lives and careers come in cycles . . . Maybe now it's your turn to give back to that mentor—to that person who gave you support, a reference, a kind word, encouragement, or a helpful critique. Perhaps now it's you who are in a position to give back: to hire . . . to recognize . . . to thank and acknowledge.*
>
> *Pay it forward, but also, pay it back! My hope for each and every one of you is that now, or ten or twenty or forty years from now, your work and the legacy you leave is acknowledged, recognized, and valued, even if it's just within a small circle . . .*
>
> *Now, as one of Dr. Seuss's characters asks: "How did it get so late so soon?"*

ACKNOWLEDGMENTS

MY STORY AS A BILINGUAL, bicultural journalist owes an immeasurable debt of gratitude to the two people who made it all possible — Charles and Adela Martin, who gave me life and so much more. To my *Abuelita Lupe* and her kind heart and all my ancestors who have given me the strength and grace to endure.

To those pioneers in bilingual broadcasting who had the vision and saw the need for media that reflected our reality. I owe them a debt of gratitude.

To the many journalists and *comunicadores sociales* whom I've had the honor to know and work with in Guatemala, Bolivia, Uruguay, Argentina, and Nicaragua — you have inspired me with your commitment in spite of the challenges you face each day. Hector Cordero, Claudia Méndez Arriaza, Carlos Dada, the late Ileana Alamilla, José Ruben Zamora — so many more, too numerous to mention. I thank all of you for your brave work and pray for your protection.

Especially, I acknowledge Selma Saravia of Bolivia for her friendship, support and great commitment to better journalism in her country — also for giving me my first assignment training journalists. A toast of *prosecco* to you!

I wish to recognize with love and light all those who have listened to and supported me — radio and online listeners, friends, students and *colegas* — in the United States, Guatemala, Bolivia, Nicaragua and elsewhere. My story would be very different, if not for you. Most especially I wish to acknowledge the help and friendship of people who over the years came into my life when I needed them most, and brought me support and strength to continue my work and my mission. I am forever grateful to all of you and hope that your kindness, generosity and friendship is returned a hundredfold.

Thanks also to the staff of the John S. Knight Fellowship at Stanford University, the International Center for Journalists, the Fulbright Foundation, Rosental Alves and the Knight Center for Journalism in the Americas, and all entities and good people that have supported my journalism training work over time.

Finally, to all of you who have played any role at all in my life's story — we are all part of the great mystery — whether it is was for good, ill, or neutral, I embrace the experience and thank you.

ABOUT THE AUTHOR

Born in Mexico, and raised in the U.S., public radio pioneer MARIA E. MARTIN lives and works in Antigua, Guatemala.

An award-winning public radio journalist, Martin has developed groundbreaking series and programs for U.S. public radio, including NPR's *Latino USA* and *Después de las Guerras: Central America After the Wars*. In September of 2015, Martin was inducted into the National Association of Hispanic Journalists Hall of Fame.

For more than a decade, Martin has directed the GraciasVida Center for Media based Guatemala and Texas — a media advocacy, production and training entity dedicated to the practice of independent journalism in the public interest in the Americas (www.graciasvida.org). Maria Emilia Martin has trained thousands of journalists in the U.S., Mexico, Guatemala, Bolivia, Uruguay, and Nicaragua.

Printed in the USA
CPSIA information can be obtained
at www.ICGtesting.com
LVHW021306311223
767841LV00016B/2212